100 STRONG RESIDENCY INTERVIEW QUESTIONS, ANSWERS, AND RATIONALES

By: Brandon Dyson, Pharm.D, BCOP, BCPS and Tony Guerra, M.HCI, Pharm.D.

ISBN: 978-0-359-24749-3

100 Strong Residency Interview Questions, Answers, and Rationales

TABLE OF CONTENTS

i

INTRODUCTION

How This Book Will Help You Now

This book will help you gain an advantage over other residency candidates. Many interviewees make avoidable mistakes. Their paper qualifications are faultless, but they don't match with the residency site because of a preventable mistake. Residency sites have more applicants than spots and they need a way to continue to pare down their list of applicants.

We're not going to waste your time. This book will be useful immediately, helping you brush up on basics and taking a deep dive into challenging questions. We felt current interview books missed an underlying rule, a principle that guided each question and interaction. Let's explain this with an exercise.

Take a moment and imagine that you've answered an interview question correctly. Now imagine another applicant with a pleasant foreign accent has answered that same question. Who is more memorable?

One gets a checkmark for the right answer, another gets an invitation to speak again. The interviewer found him or her unique.

We're not suggesting you fake an accent; we're saying that when you think you've answered something right, then you've done a *good* job. Many candidates will do a *good* job. But with only a few spots available for dozens of candidates, you'll need to do the *best* job. In fact, to keep reminding yourself to up your game, keep that pleasant foreign accent in mind.

Your biggest problem won't be getting the answers right; your biggest challenge is becoming memorable.

To avoid being forgettable and ordinary, you'll need to pause, gather your thoughts, and then answer. Respond with an answer that impresses (without boasting), is succinct but not abrupt, and is accurate but doesn't make you sound like a know-it-all. With the tips we give you, we think you'll be much better prepared. You can beat that other candidate who had that special tiebreaker, accent or other notable quality.

If You Could See the Interview from Our Side

Often I've wanted to shout "Stop the Interview" or "Time Out." I wanted to tell the applicant that he or she is either saying something wrong. I've wanted to say, "I just heard this exact answer in the interview before you." Both candidates were a top choice *before* the interview.

With the questions, answers and rationales in this book, we'll strengthen your interview prowess. You'll understand why some standard questions exist. You'll learn how to get it right when there's no right answer.

When you understand why interviewers ask certain questions and what the interviewer hopes to learn, you'll be able to give a memorable response. Interviewing for a job resembles working with patients. Understanding 'the why' helps you succeed.Let's begin with the fundamentals. If you want to get to the questions right away, that's fine, skip ahead. But, missingastep can end the game quickly.

Nine Interview Fundamentals

1. **Keep answers tight.** The interviewers have a schedule to follow, as well as specific questions to ask. If you go on tangents, you'll get a "no answer" for some questions because you took too long. Be brief, not abrupt. Describe clearly, but don't try to squeeze in an epic novel.

2. **Bring high energy.** Give your interviewer(s) the courtesy of being able to sense your excitement that says, "This is the #1 residency I want to come to." If it's not, they'll know.

3. **It's not about you.** This interview is about what you can do for them. While you want to know if you will be happy there, the time to reflect on your happiness is after the interview is over. Timing is key.

4. **You're a great teammate.** They are going to be working with you and there is always more work than there is time to do it. Are you going to be a person who steps it up? Make sure they know you are.

5. **If it's personal, keep it private.** So many people I've interviewed blurt out something that they feel is a reason for selecting them; they try to play the sympathy card. Don't make it awkward.

6. **Have someone else critique what you wear.** You might think you're rockin' it with your business attire, but what seems appropriate to you might get you noticed for the wrong reasons. It's too important not to get a second opinion. First impressions stick; make sure your initial impression is a positive one.

7. **Build a confident stance.** You may not have the stamina to maintain your posture in an all-day interview. Many jobs include hunching over and you may have chosen homework over workout. Getting to the gym and doing the rower and core strength-building exercises will help you maintain a confident posture. Exude an air of self-confidence with your posture (and a smile!)

8. **Has the interview started already?** The second you shake a hand, the interview is 'game on.' Just because you're not sitting at a conference table doesn't mean they aren't scrutinizing you. Engarde!

9. **Do your homework.** The easiest way to show you think they are number one is to research the heck out of the opportunities there. Learn about their organizational culture to make sure their expectations, philosophy and values match yours.

To help you prepare, you can pick up a free Residency/Job Evaluation Form by joining the email list at https://www.tldrpharmacy.com/

Also, you'll get the Antibiotic Cheat Sheet, and Chapter 1 of *Pharmacy School: The Missing Manual* as well.

Strong Accent? Some Strong Advice

It's important for the health care team and patients to understand you clearly. I'm a first-generation college student and while I was born in the United States, English was not my first language. I worked hard on my spoken and written skills. I've been a Toastmaster since my teens working on public speaking. I have a bachelor's degree in English because I knew how important communication was. So, what can you do if your accent is strong?

Our profession's diversity is a strength. The local pharmacist likely speaks the language of the local population. If your accent is strong, and your goal is to help that population, make sure to say so early. Patients need someone that speaks their language much more than they need someone who knows if the grammatical end of a sentence should be "him and me" or "he and I." The residents are like you. They want to help others. If your altruistic mission is clear and unique, they will get behind you, rather than put up a wall to block you. You are also more memorable.

If you have a similar accent to the interviewer, it may not matter. If you're from Boston or New York and applying to residencies in Boston and New York, they may favor you because you sound like an East Coaster. However, you want to soften your accent in other regions to ensure clear understanding. Be careful about sports teams, people are funny about that, you may connect with the Chicago fan only to find the rest of the group is from St. Louis in baseball or Green Bay in football. Ideally, people wouldn't judge you on these aspects. But, people want to work with others like themselves.

Pronunciation Errors

The Interviewers' Names

Never guess, always politely ask how to pronounce the interviewer's name if it seems like an odd spelling. It's much better to pronounce it right than to be someone who didn't care to ask.

Pronouncing Drug Names

There are variations on drug pronunciation like diazepam [die A zuh pam] versus [die ah zuh pam] that are regional which is fine.

Metoprolol as meh TOE pruh lawl versus meh tuh PRO lawl is also a variant, but the former seems more common. What's not okay are true mispronunciations.

For example, sometimes you'll hear atenol instead of atenolol or simvastin instead of simvastatin. Both are deletion errors, a syllable is missing.

If you're native language is not English, as mine wasn't, consider listening to How to Pronounce Drug Names, the audiobook.

BLOCK 1 – WARM-UP QUESTIONS

When you first meet a person at the site, you may get some informal questions as you walk down the hallway. You're in the interview! Answer thoughtfully and ask questions back. If they ask where you are from, it's polite to return that question.

Let's begin.

1. Where did you grow up?

There's no mystery about this question. Be yourself. While there's not a right answer, there are wrong answers. Don't make stories about your years as an undercover spy. You don't need a Walter Mitty life story to sound interesting. Instead, highlight what others find interesting and don't discount what *you* think isn't interesting.

For example, I come from a rural state and a person from a small town might find his or her hometown uninteresting to others. However, I was born in the Nation's Capital. I'm very interested in hearing about small town life. The interviewer might want to know about Washington, D.C. in return.

The interviewer wants to get to know you and assess your fit with the team. Being genuine to your uniqueness makes a much better impression than trying to be someone you aren't. Interviewers don't judge where you are from. They evaluate how well you articulate what makes you unique.

Also, where you get questions matters. If you hear "where did *you* grow up?" while walking down a hallway, ask back. However, if you're in the interview conference room with an audience, and they are clearly burning through a prewritten list, don't ask back.

2. What do *you* find important on your CV?

This tests how well you know your CV. Did you create a ten-page CV with everything you've ever done? Or, did you make clear what's important? Interviewers will ask about your work history, presentations, and publications. Be able answer questions on the spot.

Example questions could go like this: Tell me about that drug that you did a Medication Use Evaluation (M.U.E.) on. What did you find? What were the results? All that's fair game if it's on your CV.

The key is to briefly summarize your rotations, work history, and anything that involves transferable skills. As they ask specifics, show them you're a good fit for their program.

We cover CVs extensively in Chapter 4 of *Mastering the Match*.

3. Why do you want to do a residency?

Now we're getting to the fun stuff. I'll give a sample answer for this question beginning with "I would like to do a residency because . . .

I want to develop a skillset as I'm not sure where the field of pharmacy is going in 5, 10 or 20 years. I know I have to be adaptable to the market's needs. Even in the past few years, pharmacy has grown with immunizations and collaborative practice and potentially provider status. We can prescribe specific drugs like oral contraceptives. As the profession has grown, I need to develop a mindset and ability to teach myself to grow alongside it. That's why I want to do a residency.

What makes this answer strong is its brevity. You've created a thesis that you need a skillset. You believe the residency is one avenue to get it. Finally, you restate the question as a statement to make clear you've finished speaking. Not only does your answer make sense, but it shows you can clearly articulate a complex topic in a few sentences.

4. What drew you to our program?

The answer depends on the institution. You want to be honest and avoid a canned response. A sample answer might say:

Oncology interests me. I know this is a National Cancer Institute (NCI) accredited institution and there is an active oncology practice with inpatients and outpatients. I know you do bone marrow transplants. I've heard, just from talking with the other preceptors with whom I've interviewed, that you're looking to do CAR-T therapies here. These are cutting-edge leukemia and lymphoma treatments. I want to grow and learn in this environment. I love that you have an oncology PGY-2. Ideally, if we're a good fit, I could train as a PGY-2 here. I would love that.

You can find a comprehensive blogpost about oncology at The Ultimate Guide to Oncology Pharmacy for the Non-Oncologist at TLDRPharmacy

5. How does this program match your ideal residency?

This piggybacks off the last question. I'd answer this in two parts. First, answer the program match. Then answer the "ideal residency" half.

I said I'm interested in oncology, but it's whatever you want: transplant, critical care, ambulatory care, etc. This sample answer explicitly identifies the three parts of a good answer: 1) the thesis, 2) the evidence and 3) the conclusion.

Oncology has always interested me. (Your Thesis) Here there's an outpatient infusion center, an inpatient practice with bone marrow transplants and from what I see, a very active leukemia and lymphoma service. (Your Evidence) I want to learn in this environment. (Your Conclusion)

With the 'ideal residency' part of the question, I talk about my desire for growth, as the ideal, but clarify specific matching points. It may seem obvious, but make sure you address both 'program match' and 'ideal residency' in your response.

First, I want a program that's going to help me better develop into the best pharmacist I can be. I want to develop a clinical mindset, the ability and the skillset to teach myself to thrive in any practice environment.

Second, I'm interested in oncology as I mentioned and that subspecialty frequently changes with the research that's going on in the area. Sometimes guidelines from six months ago are not even a blip. I'm not looking to learn clinical work in this one snapshot. That won't hold water. What I want is to be around people who move flexibly with the changes and see how they do it. I feel this is a good match because in talking to past and current residents, they've been able to keep up not only during residency, but well into their careers.

6. What does working at the top of your license mean?

Uh oh, they caught you in a cliché. While it's okay to say you want to be the best, it's an amorphous term. Is the best pharmacist one who wins awards or who is remembered by the most people? Can a retail pharmacist ever be at the top of his or her license, or does he or she have to be a clinical pharmacist? Tread lightly because some of your staffing duties may include outpatient pharmacy which is similar to retail. Here's how you can turn this "gotcha!" into a well-articulated response.

I've heard the"top of the license expression," especially from my college's faculty. I think it means in some pharmacy roles, you don't necessarily need the therapeutics lectures and clinical experiences as much. A pharmacist working at the top of the license pushes the limits of responsibility allowed by the license. Boundaries we've explored include immunizations, collaborative practice, and prescribing a narrow group of medicines. The expression conveys someone has a growth mindset. I want to learn and keep up with the most current literature so I can provide the best patient care. I don't think practice environment matters as much as practice mindset.

Bam! Shoots. Scores. Now, we return to a boilerplate scripted question.

7. What short-term and long-term goals do you have?

Now, you really want to divide this into two distinct answers and answer with no more than three goals per question. You should know these ahead of time.

My short-term goals are to finish my PGY-1 residency, preferably here at this institution. I'd like to work better clinically with other practitioners. I've been on rotations for a few months. I'm growing to know my role on the team. I feel more clinically sound with each experience. I'm specifically working on patient interactions and if accepted here, I could continue to develop my skills over the next year.

Longer-term, I'm interested in a PGY-2 and actively looking now. My ideal setting is critical care. I'm not 100 percent certain whether I want to specialize in SICU or MICU or Neuro ICU. I'm not even sure if someone canspecialize between two or three settings, but I see critical care or emergency care in my future.

Down the road, I see myself as a specialist working with the team in that capacity. What I believe may make me unique is my interest in administration and process improvement. So, I see myself in clinical practice for the next five years, but potentially moving into formal leadership roles down the line.

That's often how many candidates see their future. However, one of this book's authors skipped a PGY-2 altogether. He got a call for an oncology specialist opportunity in Texas. He jumped on that chance and worked his way up to director without a PGY-2. The other author saw a pharmacist create a PGY-2 emergency medicine residency and land as residency program director. But, she never did a PGY-2 herself. While your answers should follow logical paths, know the winds may take you in a different direction. Flexibility after a well-matched PGY-1 allows you to run with it.

8. At retirement, would you have earned pens from fellow faculty?

Let's break this question into two parts: the retirement and the pop culture reference. If you understand the pop culture reference, immediately acknowledge it. Say, "I certainly would love to win a Nobel Prize, but I might find happiness in more modest accomplishments." If you don't get it, ask for the reference.

The question describes two scenes in the movie *A Beautiful Mind* with Russell Crowe. Upon winning the Nobel Prize, his colleagues dropped off pens in the faculty dining area. This symbolizes the highest honor his peers could give. Asking shows that when you don't know something, you'll ask.

Let's unpack what a "look into the future" question really asks. You're going to work with this group for at least a year. Some of the current residents may accept positions there. You want to highlight what you bring to the table for *them*. This question begs you to talk about yourself. It's an opportunity to show restraint and humility and see how well you integrate. Here's a sample response:

I'd like my colleagues to remember that I was always willing to step up, that I was a team player, and that I would cover a call in and do whatever I could. I'd like them to remember I always had a smile and a positive attitude. I was a genuinely happy person who found joy in his work and was pleasant to be around. I would definitely want a story where the entire room got to share in a laugh or two and maybe a quiet moment. Yes, I would really like that.

9. What qualities make a good resident?

This question asks you to assess your strengths and weaknesses. These are excellent questions to highlight and practice. On the Internet, this is often named the 'humble brag.' You want to talk about how great you are in a way that sounds like *"oh well, that is just that. It's nothing."* Here's a good sample answer:

First, I have a genuine desire to become an outstanding pharmacist. I know I'm not there yet, but I know how hard I'm working to get there. I look forward to learning from medical residents, nurses, my colleagues, coworkers, pharmacy techs and pharmacists. I thrive in an environment where there is so much to learn. I can't wait to learn everything that everyone can teach me.

Second, I want to help out as much as I can and become an integral part of this team. I understand there's a value I can bring to this system, and getting as much as possible out of this year means giving as much as I can. I understand the dichotomy in this relationship, and honestly, I can't wait for it. In summary, I feel I can add value to the team by working hard, being a team player and learning as much as I can.

10. Please self-evaluate your clinical abilities?

Answer this question as honestly as possible. You have weak points you want to address, and the humble brag works here. My answer would go something like this:

I'm confident with what I've learned in school. I've done well with grades, but I know many students have also succeeded. I feel I've worked hard and thrived in making the most of my rotation opportunities, but recognize it's not the real world. The real world's not a multiple-choice test nor the 9 to 5 Monday through Friday of some APPEs.

My single best skill, I think, as a future clinician, is that I'm not afraid to say I don't know something. I'll look it up and find the answer. Specifically, in ambulatory care, I felt strongest in diabetes management paired with my college's diabetes concentration. I'm working to develop skills with other chronic conditions. I had an internal medicine rotation just before my infectious disease rotation focusing on HIV. I felt I built a strong foundation. I could also see what specialist pharmacy looks like, but also how much I need to grow. How a PGY-2 graduate approaches problems and questions is very different.

Weaknesses. Well, I haven't been in a critical care environment yet or ever been one-on-one with a cancer patient in an oncology specialization. So, it's learning how the skillset I have applies to a new patient with a different pathophysiologic state. Let me ask you a question since you mentioned critical care is your specialty. I've done an internal medicine rotation and worked with internal medicine patients. Intuitively, I would think it's the same patient, just sicker. Is that true, or is it an entirely different thing?

Instead of sandwiching strengths then weaknesses and finishing by *repeating* the strengths, this final question surprises. It says, *"I'm not afraid to ask."* By saying I don't yet know the difference between internal med versus critical care patients in practice, you share the stage with the interviewer. This breaks up the one-sidedness of a line of questioning.

To make HIV a little more accessible, you can check out The Ultimate Guide to HIV for Pharmacists at TLDRPharmacy.com

BLOCK 2 – REFLECTION QUESTIONS

Before the interviewers evaluate you, they are going to ask you to assess yourself. These are questions you should have readily available but do still pause before each answer. Be thoughtful, not scripted.

11. What challenges did you have in college?

You're going to get an iteration of this question on every job interview you will ever have for the rest of your life. What are difficulties you've experienced in the past with classes, classmates, or co-workers? As a theme, honesty is vital, but this is not a confession. Saying, "*I hated transplant; it was four weeks of hell,*" is not the way to go. Instead, try this:

I had an APPE rotation in the solid organ transplant setting. It was a challenging experience, especially with the drugs. Quite honestly, I am still not sure how to make dose adjustments to tacrolimus. There were clinically intense patients in a very fast paced and demanding rotation which I found very new. I had one or two lectures on solid organ transplant back in school, and I did extra research before the rotation to try to bring myself up to speed, but wow, I really underestimated the treatment complexities.

I stayed late, asked as much as I could from the current resident and my preceptors, of course. The nurses were patient with me, and I asked where they picked up their knowledge. I found I grew a lot, not just from the content knowledge, but from approaching other health professionals for support.

12. Why did you get into pharmacy?

Each person will have his or her own story for this, and the key is to demonstrate that you are committed to the profession. Be honest. If you were premed and discovered pharmacy, you'll find a lot of heads nodding in agreement. If you found pharmacy after you lost your job in the crash, say so. But tell a story, succinctly. Here's mine:

When I was a kid, I visited a hospital with my 10-year-old friends and their parents. A Washington Post columnist happened to be there and wanted to take a picture of me, or one of my friends, for an op-ed piece. I had no idea what op-ed was at the time, and I was really shy, so my friend took the opportunity and there he was two days later, in The Washington Post as a kid dressed in scrubs like a doctor.

I remember how proud his parents were and how disappointed mine were. It's like I had really gotten an acceptance for medical school and turned it down. Later, I did think of medical school as part of getting my toe into the healthcare waters. I volunteered at a pharmacy, and my path went in that direction instead of medical school. So, I turned down becoming a physician twice in my life. The neat thing is that the other kid, the one who dressed up as a doctor, ended up as an actor. You can dress up however you like, but I've found that just being open to what will happen works best.

Note, I've mentioned Washington D.C. a couple of times, and that may actually be a good thing. I might become, in the interviewers' minds, "DC Tony." If I'm in the Maryland / DC / Virginia area searching for residencies, then they know I'm already familiar with the area, what it costs to live there, and the quirks of licensing. If I'm applying out of the area, the Washington D.C. diamond image is effortless to picture, and they can associate me with an image. Fiction authors do this all the time. They take a person, give him or her a notable feature or background characteristic, and call him or her by it. "Jersey Joe," "Maryland Mary," and "Texas Tom" are some I just made up. If you're savvy about it, you can pick a memorable but respectful nickname you have, and use it as an anchor for them to remember you out of the dozens of other candidates.

13. What were your two favorite and one least favorite clinical rotations? Why?

This is a lot to think about as it's a roundabout way of asking for your strengths and your weaknesses. It's also a well-hidden landmine on the road to residency. If you start talking about your least favorite rotation, and you use it as an opportunity to tee off on the preceptor with whom you really didn't get along, you're not answering the question correctly. Right? Remember how small the world of pharmacy is. Worse yet, the interviewer probably knows the preceptor about whom you're talking, so you really want to make sure that even if you had a problematic rotation, the onus of having a bad situation and turning it into a good one is on you. Begin with it's not your preceptor's fault or your school's fault.

The other thing you have to watch out for is where you are interviewing. If your favorite thing in the world is critical care and you're interviewing for an ambulatory residency, why are you interviewing for this residency? If you love critical care so much and this is Am Care, you may need to qualify that the preceptor there was inspirational, and so you now want Am Care as a career. Another example might be that you loved the outpatient warfarin clinic and currently you're interviewing for the inpatient specialty. You need to be clear about how a good experience has transferable skills. What then is an excellent potential answer? Start with your favorite, on a positive note.

My favorite rotation was internal medicine. The disease states were diverse, and I felt in this particular rotation that pharmacy was valued. I was able to play a critical role in patient care. We were integral, rounding with the team every day, and had the authority to make interventions. Others listened to us, asked for our input, and that was great. What I really liked about this rotation was that my preceptor gave me some autonomy. He let me round by myself some days and then I would pre work-up the patients. I'd meet them quickly before rounds and go over what I noticed and potential interventions. I liked that feeling of being on my own, but having someone to lean on.

Now, the mistake is to put in as much detail in your second rotation as your first. I don't think it's hyper-relevant and they'll get more of the same. A quick, "another favorite was my pediatric rotation" will do fine. Make sure not to say my second favorite or third favorite, because it makes it sound more negative.

Here's how I'd answer the least favorite question:

My least ideal rotation was the HIV clinic where my concerns were multifaceted. It was one of my first rotations; there were so many drugs that I had a hard time keeping up with them. It wasn't just HIV; patients had Hep-C, and there were cocktails of medications for that. Because they were immunosuppressed, you had to give them prophylactic antibiotics, and just trying to keep track was tough. There were many drug interactions we were watching including genotyping resistance panels, and I really struggled. I had a demanding preceptor, but in a lot of ways, I actually liked that. Because my interest wasn't really in that particular area of pharmacy, I had to change my thought process.

My first thought was that I had a lot to learn and while I might have preferred this rotation as more of a capstone, a challenge in my 7th or

8ᵗʰ block, I made the best of it. In the second week, I took a minute to talk to my preceptor about where I felt I was. While he didn't ease up, it seemed he respected that I was learning the lesson he wanted me to – imagining how I would feel as a patient with this many things going on with drug therapy. I really learned to empathize in a way I don't think I could have if things had been a lot easier for me. Looking back now as I talk to you, while it wasn't my favorite rotation, it certainly was one of the most impactful. I'm thankful for it, and I'm grateful I was able to turn it around.

Remember, end on a positive note!

Hep-C treatments are challenging to take on, there is a blogpost titled Hepatitis-C Treatment 101 at TLDRPharmacy.

14. What drug classes do you find the easiest and hardest?

This is another landmine. If you talk about how you're very strong with anticoagulation and you really get warfarin and apixaban, then you might get slammed with a "let's just see how well you do know those coagulation pathways" question. I'm not saying people are going to do it maliciously, but be careful talking about your strongest area; remain humble because you don't know how much experience the person on the other end of the interview table has.

It's the same with the weakest class. Don't' say "*HIV and oncology are just overwhelming; I'll never understand those.*" This interviewer has to make a judgment call on if you're going to pass the NAPLEX six months before you take the NAPLEX. So, make sure that what follows your weakest class answer is an action plan you're working on to bring your knowledge to where it needs to be.Here's a sample answer:

My strongest class, I'd say is anticoagulation; I did really well on that module in school. I'm really intrigued by the pharmacology and the drug interactions, and I appreciated that what I learned in class matched up with my time in the 'anticoag' clinic. We got to do draws and dose warfarin. It was a collaborative practice, so we got to help dose for the physicians. We did hold times for procedures. I really enjoyed it, and I learned so much, but I acknowledge that it was only a five-week experience and I've still got a long way to go. I am just really passionate about anticoagulation, and I think it's a high impact area for pharmacists.

My weakest class was definitely oncology. I feel like we barely touched it in school and there are so many drugs. I'm not confident that I could pronounce half of them. At least it feels that way. And everything's always changing. I did okay with the module in school, but I also had a rotation with oncology, an APPE rotation with an oncology pharmacist who specialized in bone marrow transplant, and I struggled. I mean I learned a lot, but still, I would say I'd have a difficult time saying a lot about it. Now that it's been two months since the rotation I'm trying to shore that up as well as some other gaps. I'm restudying my old oncology notes and poking around on the Internet. I'm looking at NCCN and ASCO and just trying to find overall summaries that might help out. And, I'm working withRxPrep to make sure I clear the NAPLEX hurdle.

If you need to brush up on anticoagulation, look toTLDRPharmacy's<u>Anticoagulants, The Definitive Guide</u>

15. Can you detail your research for us?

We need to break this into two parts: if you have done research or if you haven't. Again, be honest. If you haven't done research, don't make up something.

1. If you're going to have to say, "*I haven't done research,*" then your sample answer is brief and sounds like this.

I haven't actually had too much of an opportunity at this point to conduct any kind of research, clinical or otherwise, but that's something I'm looking forward to performing.

There is a research project that's part of the residency site's accreditation. So, you *will* be doing research. You have to act at least like you're open to it, even if it makes you cringe to think about it.

2. This will undoubtedly be on your CV if you *have* done research, but the trick to this, or the area of caution, is your ability to talk about your research. When you talk to those students at ASHP presenting their work as P4s, and there are some examples on the TonyPharmD YouTube channel, they speak articulately about their research, explaining why it was important to them and what they hoped to accomplish.

If you have done research where you did a poster presentation, or you wrote up a case report for one of your preceptors, that's fine. You need to be able to answer everything that you can about it.

While it would be nice to have peer-reviewed journal articles, here's a sample answer with what most students have, a compelling case about which they can speak intelligently.

I'd like to talk about a case report I worked on. The patient came in with an exacerbation of acutely decompensated heart failure. He was given some Lasix and developed a rash from furosemide, the only recent new drug.

After talking to him, I found he had recently rolled his ankle and had started self-medicating with ibuprofen for the pain and inflammation. He knew that he had to take ibuprofen during meals to avoid stomach upset, so he began eating four times a day instead of his usual three. When I asked about the actual meals, they were very high in sodium content. We thought the salt and ibuprofen probably exacerbated his heart failure.

Now the Lasix became part of the prescribing cascade, a medicine to treat side effects from the medication he used to self-treat his ankle injury. So, we pulled the Lasix, switched to bumetanide, and the rash resolved. We did a whole Naranjo Scale and found out that the heart failure was probably due to the Lasix. We did a literature evaluation and saw that this sort of thing wasn't new. But learning the process of solving the problem and looking to share that knowledge with others was really valuable for me.

16. What do you like about writing?

Don't lie. Seriously, just don't. If you say you love to write and you don't, you're in a heap of trouble if one of the interviewers really does. Tony majored in English as an undergrad, so he could, in a just a few questions, find out if you are or aren't much of a reader or writer. It's understandable to want to be what the interviewer wants, but the interviewer wants someone who's honest. Here's a sample response:

Writing's not my favorite, but I'm certainly willing to do it, and when I do it, I'll put into it the same energy I put into everything I do. I earned a bachelor's degree before pharmacy school, so I had many intensive humanities courses as part of the core curriculum. I also have read several medical journals, so I feel I communicate relatively clearly. I do a decent job when I write, but writing's just not my favorite thing. I know communication is a huge part of our profession, so I embrace writing when I'm teaching, and so forth, but I'm going to say there's not a novel in my future in the next decade or so.

You'll probably get a "fair enough," from the interviewer, but what you gave them was honesty and the knowledge that you are someone who is going to be straight with them.

17. What teaching experience do you have?

This question's more about learning about your hobbies and figuring out a piece of the puzzle that is you. While it would be ideal for a student to have college classroom experience, an example could sound like this, and it doesn't have to be pharmacy related:

When I was 16, I gave guitar lessons to other kids in my high school. I created some individual lesson plans, and we met every week for an hour. I believed, at least with guitar lessons, that students were going to be more inclined to practice if they learned songs that they wanted to play. I wasn't necessarily trying to have them play Mozart or Beethoven as one might with a classical piano lesson, but I taught them about the circle of fifths and music theory. I started them with "Hey, here's the Green Day song. Once you can play it, your friends will recognize it. They will think that it's cool." That inspired them, and we all had a great experience.

Since you may be saying you're interested in teaching as part of a pharmacy school, it would be good for you to know where a college professor's priorities are based on where he or she works.

A professor who works at a small liberal arts college likely has teaching as the primary goal, then service, and lastly, research. Service includes academic advising to individual students or clubs, serving on committees like admissions, or participating in local and national organizations.

Professors who work at large research universities, especially early in their careers, must focus on research, the "publish or perish" expression, then service, and lastly, teaching. That may seem strange to you because what you, as a student, usually see is the person in the classroom. However, when you have a one-on-one or are on a research team with a professor, you are able to see just how good they are.

Professors, like Tony who is one of the authors of this book, who teach at community colleges, perform teaching and service without regard to a research component. In pharmacy school where a professor might teach one class in the fall and two in the spring, the professor would be teaching '1 plus 2'. Tony teaches four classes in the fall and four classes in the spring, so he teaches '4 plus 4'. In fact, he has an academic APPE rotation where P4s get in front of students for face-to-face teaching for four days a week. This provides them the opportunity to be able to talk about their genuine college teaching experience.

18. What is your teaching philosophy?

This will be a difficult question for you to answer if you have no teaching experience, but we'll prepare you for this question here. Most teachers write a teaching philosophy statement; it's one to two typewritten pages, on how they work to be effective teachers. We've known some pharmacy students who were middle school or high school teachers before they enrolled. They might have one written down. But, unless you've done an Academic APPE, you probably won't have a teaching philosophy. Most develop their teaching philosophy while earning a teaching certificate *in* residency.

There's a hidden agenda with this question, and they want to know if you're going just make something up to try to sound like you know what you're talking about. That's not a good idea for pharmacists in general. You never want to make up answers when you're talking about medications and dealing with people's health and wellness. The same is true with this question. What shows a lot of maturity and preparation is if you have a teaching philosophy statement that reflects how you teach patients without having had formal academic classroom experience. Either way, be honest.

You might answer like this if you've never taught but tutored a little.

I don't have extensive teaching experience. I mentioned the guitar lessons in an earlier question, and based on that, I would say my philosophy is to find common ground with students. With guitar, I know it's ideal for a student to learn music theory. I recognize how beneficial it is to learn scales, but that's not fun to practice or play.

Maybe I can meet the student at his or her level and teach him or her how to play a cool song. I'll reverse things to teach the student music theory and scales from that song.

It would be the same with pharmacy and how I tutored pharmacology for a classmate in pharmacy school. I tried to relate to the student's goals as a specific practitioner. He was interested in pediatrics so I gave him a calculations example with a pediatric patient to contrast it with that of an adult patient. I showed him a bit of what would be coming and how he would be able to apply it in practice.

Both of these examples are reasonable explanations of how you would teach, but don't require that you have had formal teaching experience.

19. How will you fit teaching in? You'll be busy.

This is a question about prioritizing and organizing. Obviously, you are going to be extraordinarily busy as a resident. You'll probably precept students, especially if you're getting a teaching certificate, and you'll want to be prepared. Here's how you might answer the question even if you've never taught.

I'll start with the expression that "if you lose an hour in the morning, you'll look for it all day." I want to tell a quick story about a resident who always made sure she didn't lose that hour. I appreciated the residents who took the time to teach me. I know how busy residents are just from my own rotations so far. I had one particular resident who's become a mentor to me. She went through what she was assigned to do, but also shared additional background literature in this Am Care clinic. I felt so much more prepared to meet with patients as I started to understand why we would take a particular approach. I want to mentor as she did.

I mean, yes, it requires more work, but her method was to come to work a little early, not always an actual hour, to set up a teaching system so she didn't reinvent the wheel. She said it took a lot of time at first, but with that system, it made it possible for her to teach more, much faster. What I think worked as well is that when as students we saw how much energy they were putting in, we reciprocated, trying our best to give back by staying a bit later ourselves. She could have focused on her longitudinal projects, but it was clear she had a calendar for taking care of those a little at a time. I learned and appreciated not only the content I learned but how she prioritized and organized her activities.

20. What qualities does your model preceptor have?

This is a good question because it's self-reflective. Answering it well shows you've thought about it. It's a window into what you like and what you don't, similar to a trick question. You don't want your ideal preceptor to hold your hand the entire time. For example, "*she rounded with me every day, and I felt very safe.*" Or that she kept *you* accountable rather than you demonstrating your autonomy and self-motivation. "*She made sure we worked up every single patient together and had every detail before rounds, and she was always on rounds with me. Sometimes the patients would ask me questions, but mostly they would ask her.*"

Even if you did learn a lot by observing, that's not going to be a model preceptor. Also, if it is what you liked, that's not the answer you want to give on your residency interview. Remember, the goal of your residency is to get you to become that model preceptor.

The goal is to turn you from a passive to an active practitioner who rounds making his own or her own recommendations. The interviewers want to know they'll be able to take a day off from time to time because they trust you. You can still pay homage to the preceptor who sheltered you but articulate how you asked to spread your wings slowly. You might have had to ask for autonomy, but you developed into someone who worked on his or her own, and that's what matters. Here's an example:

I had an unexpected change in my schedule and landed in an internal medicine rotation. My rotations got shifted several weeks before, and it wasn't due to my institution or me; it just happened, so I rolled with it. I ended up being with a preceptor I didn't know and who didn't really know me and it turned out he was going to be gone for the fourth rotation week in a five-week block. Luckily, I had several rotations that fed well into this internal medicine one. I had built background skills, had hospital experience in psych, and had a good feel for things.

What I appreciated about this preceptor was how he showed me his process for working up patients. He introduced me to the computer system, the nurses, the attending, medical residents, and medical students. I really felt oriented, for lack of a better word. He showed me where I could work so I could hang out on the unit and made me feel like part of the family. He did it all during the first week. Every week he met with me to check on things we could improve and to discuss how we would apply them the next week. This feedback was phenomenal.

What I enjoyed the most was that he let me round by myself when he was gone the fourth week. He put the unit in my care. Obviously, he had a pharmacist following up, so I had someone with whom I could ask questions and who was a resource. I worked on my patients and rounded with the team, so I had autonomy. My preceptor trusted me enough to allow it, and it became the first experience where I honestly felt like a pharmacist. I want to recreate that for my students. That was really special for me.

BLOCK 3 –REFLECTIONS CONTINUED

Here are ten more questions that ask you to take the time to see what you want. They're not trying to trick you, they're trying to see if you took the time to see if residency was for you or if this is something you feel like you have to do. Be honest, the road moves both ways. If you're a great candidate, they're going to try to persuade you to join them.

21. What's your perfect residency?

Most candidates are going to answer this question and make it all about them. While that's important, it becomes cliché. My perfect residency becomes like a billiards shot; it sets up the next shot and the one after that so you can win the game. It sounds like this, "*my perfect residency is going to set me up for a PGY-2 or a specific future career. I'm going to learn a lot clinically and grow as a practitioner.*"

This is not a bad answer, but if you want to stick out a little bit in a good way, the real way to focus is to look at your residency, not as a way of fulfilling your pharmaceutical destiny, but as a transformation from student to practitioner. Increasing your autonomy and wearing your big boy or big girl shoes, so to speak, is the way that you achieve that. Here's how I'd answer it.

When I look in the mirror now, I see a student. My goal this next year is to move up from where I am. Clinically, I'm somewhat timid, not really sure of what I know. I'm a little uncomfortable on rounds, unsure of when to make an intervention or speak up if I notice a drug issue and when to let it slide. My ideal residency gives me the autonomy to know by the end of this residency, in any given scenario, whether in a solid organ transplant ward of a hospital or diabetes clinic, how to be adaptable. I want to be able to grasp any opportunity that comes my way. The autonomy I get from this residency will help me develop a skill set and ability to teach myself any clinical scenario in any clinical area, so that when the opportunity comes, I can take advantage of it. I want to see myself as a confident practitioner by the end of this residency.

22. What characteristics does your perfect residency have?

We've hinted at this a few times and I might include something like:

I'd love a residency that provides increasing autonomy, helps develop a clinical mindset through challenges, and where I can be part of a family. I want a residency program where I can contribute and be part of a team for a year here.

Most people don't answer it that way. It becomes a checklist that they are shopping for X, Y, and Z and it's all about them and their professional growth. Spinning it as a benefit to the hospital or clinic distinguishes you as outward thinking.

So, here's a more detailed sample answer:

Here are three things I'm really looking for. First, I want to transition from student to pharmacist in every way both mentally and physically, and to develop with everything that entails. Second, I'd like to be set on a course for continued professional growth to keep up with guidelines and be able to teach myself "how to fish," so to speak. Third, I'd really like to be part of the family here. I'd like to contribute. I really want to get to know everybody and hopefully develop lasting friendships. I'm going to spend a lot of time here and it would mean a lot to me to be an integral part of the family.

23. What challenges do you see if you were accepted here?

Be honest, but avoid "I'm scared about having to do too much work" because obviously every residency is going to have that. Saying things like that make you sound lazy.

Let's say you're interviewing in a large metropolitan area and you're from, a rural area. You might say:

I've visited big cities, but I've never lived in a city for a long time outside of a vacation week. This is the year I have the opportunity to do that. I'm a runner and I see myself pacing around the National Mall; I hear it's a little over four miles, so that excites me to be able to do that a few early mornings a week.

Spin to a positive and be specific. I've always wanted to visit this place, go to this place, and know this other place in the city. It shows you're interested and have taken the time to explore ahead of time. While it may be out of your comfort zone, the interviewer should feel good that you are pushing, but not scared you're not going to survive.

24. What do you think a residency day looks like?

This is probably a good question where you can slide in a joke to let the interviewers know that you're human. You might say something like:

I'd stroll in at 9:00 or 9:30 and get myself a Venti Starbucks now that I'm making big money. Once I hang up my coat I'd maybe get on my laptop, check CNN, and see what's going on with the world. Once I'm done with that I'd check on my patients, see what's going on in the unit. I'd grab a bite to eat and then kind of have the afternoon. You know, I mean obviously patient issues are first of course, but I'd want to devote some time to my longitudinal process project, my research project, something like that.

Again, smirk or do something to highlight you're kidding with an answer like that or you just lost the interview right there. But here's how I'd keep going.

I'd expect that in wintertime, I'll be arriving when it's dark and leaving when it's dark, except on weekends when I might just catch the rays of a sunset. I expect I'll be here between six and seven, depending on what rotation I'm on. I'll work up my patients if I'm rounding in the hospital. If I'm in an outpatient clinic I'll be tied to the hours of the clinic, but I'll be here early to work up the patients. If I do have any extra time, maybe from patient cancellations, I'd spend it on projects, reading assignments, and precepting students.

25. Did you miss out on a rotation you really wanted?

Not every student gets to actually pick how their rotations go as some are in a lottery and they get what's handed to them. This question is a way of asking what you're interested in. Be honest. If you don't know that you want to be an oncology pharmacist or pediatric care specialist or whatever, just say something like:

I'm still a fourth-year student, and every year of pharmacy school has been like peeling back the layers of an onion. I learn more about what I can do with my degree and more about "off the beaten trail" ways you can serve as a pharmacist. I'm very open to doing anything. In my rotation schedule, I wanted to make sure I saw critical care, but that I was also prepared for it by not having it as my first block. At this point in my young career, I'm very open to exploring any setting that pharmacy has for me.

26. What is a pharmacy leader's most important quality?

Okay, here's how to not answer this question. Do not list off buzzwords, like the standard jargon: honesty, integrity, passion for patient care. Basically, if your answer translates in Latin to a college's motto, you have strayed from a good answer. And please, don't say "as part of the most trusted profession, I lead from a place of . . . blah, blah, blah." Like I'm falling asleep as I'm saying this. You will not stand out.

Sure, leaders need to be honest, but what really separates pharmacists from other professionals is our ability to communicate between physicians, nurses, patients, and families. I think you should focus on that. The physician says furosemide, the nurse Lasix, the patient "water pill" and the family asks if we can get him off it because he gets up to pee at night. And we do these translations off the top of our head. But we also need to advocate for the profession; we need to get in front of people that have very little time, like senators and representatives, so public speaking is essential. I'd answer in this way:

I think communication is essential; it's not a checkbox. I continue to develop my communication through Toastmasters, a group I joined during winter break last year. I was nervous about public speaking, but knowing how much I need to be able to communicate, I decided to formalize my improvement. At these Toastmaster meetings, we have the chance to lead as the public speaker, but also to teach and comment on others' public speaking. It's helped me with an elective I'm taking online with my college this semester on cultural competency. It's one thing to communicate clearly in one's own language, but being an effective practitioner in multiple languages is something I definitely aspire to. So to answer your original question in a sentence, a leader's most important quality is a continuous commitment to improving communication.

27. How do you handle change?

Even if you dread change, this is one place to avoid being brutally blunt about your aversion to the ebbs and flows of the tides. It's really tough to know what's coming at you on a given day and if you are set in your ways, it's going to be a long road. Our profession changes rapidly and so will your residency day. This is not the time to try to win points sharing electronic health record conversion war stories. I'd address the question like this:

I'm very adaptable and try to pick up new ways of doing things. I know there are going to be hiccups whenever a new system or process rolls out, but complaining about it not only gets us nowhere, but it impacts patient care. I think we grow from change, even if it is difficult. I don't know exactly what will be there after this residency year, but I know if I'm adaptable, flexible, and can teach myself new things, I'll be ready.

28. What other programs are on your radar?

Some people look at this as a shady question to ask. I don't. I think it's them asking what kind of programs you're interested in. Your answer needs to be congruous. What I mean is that if you're sitting there interviewing for an Am Care residency, then your next stop is a Level One Trauma center focus and then Critical Care, it seems like you are casting a wide net for any old residency. What you need to be able to do is tie them together to a common theme. For example, while Am Care and Community residencies are not the same, there is a level of overlap. You can also call it exploratory since you want to see what each looks like in person. Your answer might go something like this and I'll use my own personal experience here:

Well, I've interviewed at program X, then Y, and most recently Z. I knew that I wanted to stay local and that it was important to me to do my residency in Washington, D.C. or the surrounding areas. While that might be bad advice for most people, I had a family and a setup in D.C. that I wasn't ready to leave. I only interviewed at D.C. programs which were all basically down the street.

Again, just be honest. I don't think it's a shady question, but be prepared to answer it. If you pause like someone just asked for your social security number, they may start to think you have trust issues.

29. Tell us about your strengths and weaknesses.

It's a "be honest" question, but you want to do this in a very specific way. You don't want to come across as conceited or cocky and this question is never a checkbox. Character development for both strengths and weaknesses is always an ongoing thing. It's not like, "Oh, honey, guess what? I've got character today. That's nice dear." You're never done. When you answer these questions, think about what you're good at. It might sound like this.

For my strengths, I work very well with others, I'm adaptable, and comfortable under pressure. Can I get better? Absolutely, it's an ongoing thing.

For weaknesses, stay away from the negative for too long, keep it short and sweet.

If I make a mistake, even though I learn from it, I find it difficult to forgive myself and come out of it right away. It's something I'm working on. As I currently sit, those are my strengths and a weakness.

By making them somewhat short, you beg for them to ask follow up questions. But they are asking now for more information, so it doesn't sound like you are droning on about your strengths.

30. What's one thing you would change about yourself?

This piggybacks off strengths and weaknesses. The crux here is that your answer shows what you've done and are currently doing to change that thing. They aren't asking how you're going to lose an extra fifteen pounds, deal with sleeping in when you need to be somewhere or that you drink too much. This should be pharmacy related and I might answer this way:

I get in my own head about what I know and don't know and second guess myself. Too many times I've done this on tests and it affects me. If I make a mistake, I can't recover from it easily, but it doesn't completely shut me down like it used to. I've gotten way better at it. In the little league championships when I was nine, I tried to steal third and got caught in a pickle between shortstop and third base and was tagged out. That one play stayed with me the rest of the day, so it's been with me for a while. I've found there's some benefit to this in that I work very hard not to make the same mistake twice. I learn from them quickly now and move on.

BLOCK 4 – CLINICAL QUESTIONS

You can't prepare for everything and you have no idea what they're going to ask you, but you are almost guaranteed clinical questions. The key rules of thumb for answering clinical questions are: 1) Not to make things up ever; it's okay to say I don't know and 2) If you don't know at all, know where to find the information

If someone comes in and he or she is septic, and the culture is growing Gram-positive cocci clusters, and you don't know what to do or if you have to consider for MRSA or not, you want to walk through your thought process with all of these clinical questions. There's not one right answer because the questions are designed to test your critical thinking ability.

When you notice Gram-positive cocciclusters growing, maybe you remember that's a Staph infection and that's the only thing you remember. But how do you know which strain? Is it methicillin-resistant staph (MRSA) or methicillin- sensitive Staphylococcus aureus(MSSA)? That's where you can start saying, I'm not sure in this way:

I don't remember based off of this patient's history if I have to cover for MRSA, so I would check the IDSA guidelines and the antibiogram here to see what agent has the best coverage.

These questions evaluate your critical thinking and problem-solving skills, but make sure to pick up the free Antibiotic Cheat Sheet by joining the email list at https://www.tldrpharmacy.com/ to help you better prepare.

31. Tell us about a journal club experience.

You have to know everything on your CV as we mentioned earlier. What you're really doing is giving an elevator pitch for the journal club.

I led a journal club on the TIGERS trial(fictional) in my (insert name) journal club. Basically, what it revealed was that this drug compared to this other drug was non-inferior. What was most telling was that the researchers expected the drug to be inferior.

But as you speak you really need to focus on the strengths and weaknesses of that journal article, which is the main purpose for forming a journal club. Can you apply these results from a population of 175 mostly white males to a patient population of Asian females? You can say, "*I found as I work primarily with Asian females, I can apply this to my practices.*" Think a lot about the discussion piece as it relates to strengths and weaknesses,and then whether or not you agree with them. Again, there's not a right or wrong answer.

If you want to see how a journal club works, check out the TLDRPharmacy journal club about <u>rivaroxaban with or without aspirin in stable cardiovascular disease</u> (COMPASS).

32. Tell us about a presentation experience.

Again, there's no right or wrong answer, but you'd better know every single detail if you presented on the topic. This can get tricky because you may have done a presentation on diabetes, but you'll be doing a different presentation for your residency interview.

While you may not get asked any questions after you give your spiel, be able to speak intelligently abouteverything you've presented on that's in your CV.

There is a caveat, however. If the presentation was about a clinical area, be able to talk about:

1. Landmark trials that led to the current guidelines
2. A bit about those guidelines
3. How they might change
4. What may come into the pipeline and
5. When the next guidelines might be published.

33. How do you triage clinical issues?

This is another standard job interview question where you'll get asked, "Who goes first?" especially if you work in customer service. It's about recognizing the acuity of situations. A sample scenario might be:

A patient has come in with a broken leg and you need to do his admit and med rec todetermine if he's opiate naïve so that the doctors can prescribe the appropriate pain medication. Meanwhile you're covering the code pager and a code blue signal is dispatched for an emergency on the third floor, in the medical ICU. As you're standing there, a patient's family member from a neighboring bay in the ED asks you a question about that patient. How do you prioritize your responses?

You have to recognize the acuity of the situation andI'd consider saying this:

I'm assuming there's no one else to cover the code blue emergency since I have the pager. I'd go up to the third floor in response to the code blue alert after very quickly askingnearbystaff members to find personnel who would be able to answer the family member's question and complete the med rec order.

34. Wait, you actually have two code blues.

This comes back to delegation and your acuity. You probably haven't been through many codes, but if you've ever been through one, you know that there comes a point in the procedure where your role in pharmacy is relatively complete since the patient has more or less stabilized. You can watch the EKG monitor to see if the patient's going to need amiodarone or to see what's coming next in the progression. You could argue that the initiation of the code blue situation is most important for a pharmacist. Your answer might sound like this:

I'm going to assume for the purposes of answering this question, that there are enough other people around to give compressions. I'm also going to assume there's another nurse who's available and able to take over the crash cart during the first code once the entire code team is available. After the entire team has arrived at the sight of the first code, I would run up to administer to the second code blue situation.

35. How do you treat a hypotensive patient?

Now we're getting into clinical challenges where there's not necessarily one right answer. Here's a good answer to this question that will showcase your critical thinking.

I'd first look for the source of the patient's hypotension. That might require a bit of background work outside of the scope of a pharmacist. Specifically, as a pharmacist, I would obtain and review his medication list to see if he's on any alpha blockers, beta blockers, or less likely, tricyclic antidepressants. I would do my best to contribute in that way and suggest with the team if I suspected any of his medications could have been the cause.

I'm assuming, depending on his history, that we might be checking blood cultures to see if he's septic. He might just be dehydrated. Maybe he needs some saline. Is chest pain accompanying the hypotensive attack? I can have a role, but it's not my role to decide to give him a liter of saline. However, if he's hypotensive because he's septic, I could help with empiric antibiotic selection.

So, it's really about assessing what is and isn't a pharmacist's role, and articulating how you would ascertain probable causes.

36. What do you do for a patient subtherapeutic on a parenteral or oral anticoagulant?

Your answer is going to be along the lines of what have you done so far. Really, this is about asking questions as much as answering the posed one.

Let's assume we're using warfarin and enoxaparin for argument's sake. Have we moved the warfarin dose? Where do we start him? You're probably not an expert at dosing warfarin, so they're not expecting an answer that demonstrates you are. The key is not to say, "*I haven't done Coumadin clinic so I have no idea.*" Rather, think fundamentals. The wrong answer is discontinuing enoxaparin because it's been five days; he needs coverage because he's subtherapeutic. So, keep the enoxaparin and then start recounting the questions you'd pose.

Is this patient warfarin resistant? Does he need a higher dose?

It's still five days, right? It takes a full week for a dose of warfarin to really run its course, so to speak. So, it's still early.

We may not have to do anything.

Is the warfarin 1.9 where you just keep the warfarin dose the same or is it 1.2 where we probably need to tweak the warfarin dose?

Answer it in a vague way that demonstrates what you do know, but include what you still need to ask through good critical thinking. There is a TLDRPharmacy.com blog post called Anticoagulants: The Definitive Guide that you should definitely check out.

37. What do you do for a severely hypokalemic patient?

Your job as a pharmacist is to make sure that the patient gets supplemental potassium and that you understand sliding scale potassium. Distinguishing between IV potassium and oral supplementation is key if the patient starts developing symptoms, experiences changes in his heart rhythm,or has other hypokalemia signs or symptoms. Remember with clinical questions, especially if you don't know the full answer and can't give a complete summary of the treatment of a given disease state, focus on the clinical process.

Most practicing pharmacists can't answer everything off the top of their heads. But you should know the role of a pharmacist in this situation. Your answer might be a series of questions like this:

I would assess the patient's med list. Are there drugs that can cause hypo? Is the patient on diuretics? Is there a large furosemide dose on board or was there a recent medication change?

Show your knowledge with a clear demonstration of the pharmacist's role. By the way, since residency directors may be looking to this book for some questions, and might think to change this to a hyperkalemia case to throw you off. There is a wonderful TLDRPharmacy.com blog post Hyperkalemia: An Overview for Pharmacists.

38. What would concern you about a birth control prescription and St John's Wort?

Generally speaking, if you get a drug interaction question, it's probably a trap. The default answer is that you're concerned, and you'd better be absolutely sure you are 100% correct if you have *no concerns* in this example.

Let's first pretend you don't know the interaction; your first step is to say, "*I would look for interactions in Lexicomp or Micromedex.*" While you might think they're going to be displeased if they don't hear St John's Wortinduces CYP3A4, CYP2C9 and CYP2C19 which could lead to birth control failure, there is an answer that is much more impressive and less forensic.

It seems like the patient is self-treating depression.First,I would want to look in her med history to see if she is on any other antidepressants.If she's not, then I would wonder if the patient is unable to afford mental health care. I know St. John's Wort affects the CYP pathways and there is an interaction, but I'm concerned about this patient's wellbeing and her ability to get the medicine she needs.

39. What concerns you about same class drug substitutions?

Start by elucidating a few standard facts. We have to worry about dosing and the tolerability of certain drugs. Are we talking about ACE inhibitors which are considered to be more or less equally effective? I would answer like this:

I would look to a preferred agent on the patient's insurance for affordability, but also be mindful of adherence. Is this captopril TID? Is there a generic available or only a brand? Does the drug have a narrow therapeutic index in a switch from brand Synthroid to generic levothyroxine? Sure, they're bioequivalent, but they're different enough in the given patient that you have to account for that, and potentially monitor.

The key is to demonstrate your thinking processby using a few concrete examples.

40. A patient has an INR twice as high as normal; what do you do?

In some ways, this is a "do you look at the patient, the numbers, or both?" question. This is how you make sure to cover the answer.

Certain foods and drinks affect the INR and I would look for changes in diet or medication. Doe the patient eat a lot of salads or more grilled meat and less salad? Did they increase their alcohol intake? Are there no signs and symptoms of bleeding? If so, we'd likely tell the patient to hold the dose that night and have him return to the clinic the next day.

They want to see that you look at the patient as well as the numbers.

For more on dosing warfarin check out TLDRPharmacy.com for The Pharmacy Students Guide to Dosing Warfarin Part I

BLOCK 5 – CLINICAL QUESTIONS CONTINUED

One specific kind of clinical question will not be a question at all, but rather will be a list, either in case study form or not. The interviewers are not trying to be mean or lazy; they are just trying to make sure each interviewee has about the same number and types of questions. While you might think the first step is to review the case studies, you'll have to know your pharmacology first. The first four questions in this section are really about seeing if you can sort drugs by their prefixes, suffixes, and/or characteristics. If you can, great. If not, pharm may be where you'll need to start reviewing rather than diving right into therapeutics.

41. Pharm 5 Part I – Same suffix - What are fluoxetine, duloxetine, paroxetine, atomoxetine, and vortioxetine for?

This is one of the dreaded list questions. Either verbally, or by handing you a small piece of paper, the interviewers test your knowledge of the basic sciences. Pharmacology is one of the easiest to check because they are just asking you what a drug's for. All five of the chosen drugs have the same ending, and you might think they are all for depression, which is not the case. If they give you this verbally, it's a good idea to write down the names to provide you with a better shot, and even a little time to work through your mental formulary. All of these drugs had the same –oxetine suffix, but aren't all from the same drug class. Here's the answer:

Fluoxetine (Prozac) and Paroxetine (Paxil, Paxil CR) are two of the original SSRIs generally prescribed for depression. Vortioxetine is also for depression, but it's one of the newer drugs. Its brand name actually changed from Brintellix to Trintellix because of Brintellix's similarity to Brilinta, the brand name for ticagrelor. Duloxetine (Cymbalta) is an SNRI, also for depression, but with the norepinephrine addition. Atomoxetine (Strattera) is for ADHD; it helps with cognition.

If you're not the strongest at pharmacology, or don't have a good grasp on drug endings and mnemonics, check out Memorizing Pharmacology: A Relaxed Approach to better memorize the Top 200. If you want advanced mnemonics, you'll want to check out Memorizing Pharmacology Mnemonics, to learn 450 drugs and many of the critical clinical pearls that go with them. Both are available in print, as an eBook, and as an audiobook.

42. Pharm 5 Part 2 – Similar suffix - What are omeprazole, esomeprazole, fluconazole, aripiprazole, and metronidazole for?

This list question hits you with drugs that have the same last five letters but *don't* actually all have the same suffix. Beginner health profession students look at the azole, a-z-o-l-e, and think they are similar. But once you've arrived in organic chemistry, you realize an "azole" is just a functional group. Here's the answer:

Omeprazole (Prilosec) and esomeprazole (Nexium) are proton pump inhibitors for hyperacidic states. Their stem is –prazole, p-r-a-z-o-l-e. Fluconazole (Diflucan) is an "azole" antifungal, but its actual suffix is –conazole, c-o-n-a-z-o-l-e to differentiate it from the PPIs. Aripiprazole (Abilify) is for schizophrenia or bipolar, and its suffix is –piprazole, p-i-p-r-a-z-o-l-e. The World Health Organization frowns on that suffix because it includes the PPI suffix. Metronidazole (Flagyl) is an antiprotozoal, for peptic ulcer disease or C. Diff superinfections with the –nidazole, n-i-d-a-z-o-l-e stem.

While colleges of pharmacy say you shouldn't memorize and that it's all about clinical cases and higher order thinking, there are some things that you should know because you're a pharmacist. Remember, the interviewers need to evaluate if you're going to pass the NAPLEX. If you don't know what drugs are for, how can you possibly pass a clinically based licensure exam?

43. Pharm 5 Part 3 – Same prefix - What are ceftaroline, cefepime, cephalexin, cefuroxime, and ceftriaxone for?

This list question hits you with similar prefixes, so they're expecting you know these as cephalosporin antibiotics. Now, they are asking what happens as you move up the generations. This question works with antipsychotics, antihistamines, beta-blockers and so on. They're not expecting you know the exact coverage, but that you can order them by generation and give the general trend. Here's how you might answer using the mnemonics from *Memorizing Pharmacology*:

I'd first order these from first to the fifth generation starting with cephalexin, then cefuroxime, ceftriaxone, cefepime, and ceftaroline. I remember ceph as the first generation because it has the archaic ceph, c-e-p-h. I remember the o-x, ox in cefuroxime to remember the second generation with two letters; the tri, t-r-i, for ceftriaxone, third generation; the four letters pime, p-i-m-e for cefepime; and the five-letter tarol, t-a-r-o-l, for ceftaroline, the fifth generation. In general, Gram-negative coverage, beta-lactamase resistance, and CSF penetration improves as you go up the generations.

In *Memorizing Pharmacology*, you would also learn about the antipsychotics which reduce EPS but increase metabolic effects from the first to the second generation. The antihistamines reduce sedation as you go up the generations. The beta-blockers increase beta selectivity from first to second and add a vasodilating component from second to third. Ironically, retail pharmacy students tend to have larger memorized drug formularies because most hospitals have a formulary, limiting the student's exposure to many drugs in the Top 200.

44. Pharm 5 Part 4 – Different Suffixes - What are lisinopril, valsartan, metoprolol, verapamil, and furosemide for?

Now you have different suffixes but in the same general pathophysiologic state. You may have heard of the ABCD mnemonic for cardiac drugs where A is for ACEIs, ARBs, and alpha-blockers; B is for beta-blockers; C is for calcium channel blockers; and D is for diuretics. You can add a little note about each showing that you know where these drugs fit in the individual classes. Here's how you might answer using some help from *Memorizing Pharmacology Mnemonics*:

Lisinopril has the pril, p-r-i-l, ending, that's an angiotensin converting enzyme inhibitor or ACEI. Valsartan, the ARB is an angiotensin II receptor blocker. Both of these are in the renin-angiotensin-aldosterone system, RAAS, so I'd be concerned about that duplication. Metoprolol with the –olol, o-l-o-l, ending is a second-generation beta-blocker, a good choice if the patient had an asthma component avoiding beta-2 blockade. The calcium channel blocker verapamil is a non-dihydropyridine that vasodilates and affects the heart so there might be some overlap with the beta-blocker, which is a concern. Furosemide is a loop diuretic which can deplete potassium, so I'd want to watch for that.

While it seems like a challenging and somewhat comprehensive coverage, as a 4th-year pharmacy student in February, these should easily roll off of your tongue. MedEd101.com has a weekly podcast called Real Life Pharmacology that can help you keep up.

45. How do you approach an unneeded medication in med rec?

If the interviewer doesn't have an example, it would be good for you to offer one like this:

I've seen patients on docusate sodium and Senna come to the hospital, yet they have no GI complaints. I find that in their record, they had a past injury for which they were treated with opioids, but the anti-constipation medications were never discontinued. I would work with the patient and provider to make sure they don't need these medications anymore.

A patient might have been prescribed an acute pneumonia treatment like levofloxacin, but still have that medication on his or her med list three months later. So, the team might restart the patient on levofloxacin unnecessarily and incorrectly. Be familiar with the pitfalls that come with med rec as there are often some common themes.

There is an excellent TLDRPharmacy.com post aptly named How to Do a Medication Reconciliation

46. Which HIV drug classes require renal adjustments?

This is a test of common pharmaceutical knowledge. If you say "none," then that says you didn't get the most surface information about this drug class. If you're saying, I want to do a PGY-1 and then a PGY-2 in HIV, then you should know NRTIs have renal dose adjustments.

The interviewers can probably ask the same question about a lot of the antibiotics, and it's easier to think about the exceptions rather than trying to memorize them all. For example, you know you're not going to be looking at IDSA to see if vancomycin requires a renal dose adjustment. If there is an antibiotic, it probably needs adjustment. While your NAPLEX might not be until after graduation, you want to prepare during APPEs because it helps you become competent for these questions. But you don't need to answer this if you can't list it off the top of your head and can answer this way:

I know what resources to use for HIV medications beyond the package insert. I could checkLexicomp, Micromedex, orEpocrates, but they have their own characteristics. Can I pull out my app so I can find the information?

Your ability to use clinical resources matters. Saying you can look it up right now gives them an opportunity to see you in action.

TLDRPharmacy.com has a blog post titled *Kidney Beans, Renal Function, and Drug Dosing Part I*that can give you a more comprehensive look at renal adjustments.

47. What medications would concern you in an elderly patient's profile?

Immediately, you should think Beers criteria. Note, it's neither a single light beer's criteria (the incorrect apostrophe between the "r" and "s") nor is it a six pack's criteria (no capital B). I'll get off my grammar horse now.

It will serve yourself better by answering this question in a more general way, by class, rather than single drugs.It can be brief like this:

We should at least be cautious with our anticholinergics: the first-generation antihistamines, the tricyclic antidepressants, and with benzodiazepines and sedatives in general. I'd watch for sedating muscle relaxants and opioids that might precipitate falls.

If you are relatively familiar with the criteria, you might add some notes about the updates.

I know there have been some updates to the criteria. For example, antipsychotics are out as first-line for delirium as they aren't necessarily proven effective. We try to avoid going over 8-weeks for PPIs unless there's something like Barrett's esophagus. Avoid digoxin over a daily .125 mg dose for anything in the elderly.

48. What can cause QT prolongation other than drugs?

As a pharmacist, it's essential to keep a mental list of QT prolongation drugs. But what about the NON-drug causes of QT prolongation? We don't think about them much in our profession, so this question evaluates whether you know of any. It also allows the interviewers to observe your comfort level and let them know if you will improvise an answer you don't know.

I'd answer it like this:

I'm not sure of all the things that can prolong the QT interval since a lot of my training has been drug-focused. But I can guess at a few. I know that there is a congenital QT prolongation, so for some people, there is a genetic component. I would also guess that electrolyte abnormalities such as potassium and magnesium would be a potential cause. And I would look this up to verify, but I'd imagine that recent trauma or surgery could cause arrhythmia in general, and possibly QT prolongation.

Again, the goal isn't to recite guidelines off the top of your head. It's to show your thought pattern. It's okay to guess, just make sure to indicate that you're hypothesizing and that you know where you'd look this information up.

49. How can you convey the 4 lifestyle modifications to a hypertensive patient?

This is such a significant impact area for community and ambulatory care pharmacists, that you likely know this off the top of your head. But even if you don't, remember that diet and exercise are essential to managing any chronic disease state.

Additionally, the hypertension guidelines were updated recently, so this question is a proxy to see if you keep up with the literature. You could answer this question as follows:

Diet and exercise are essential components in the treatment of most chronic diseases. With hypertension specifically, the DASH diet has been found to be particularly useful, since it places an emphasis on sodium restriction. Regular exercise is also essential, as are weight-loss management, and stress management.

You can learn more about hypertension from the TLDRPharmacy article Hypertension, A TLDRPharmacy Overview

50. How can we prevent inpatient and outpatient Adverse Drug Reactions (ADRs) and medication errors?

This question tests to see if you've been paying attention to your commissions and omissions class and also determines if you know about the Institute for Safe Medication Practices (ISMP). This is useful information because if you follow ISMP, there's a good chance you're aware of common dispensing mistakes that pharmacists make, and how to prevent them. You don't need to be a medication safety expert, but you've probably heard of at least a few. Make sure your answer reflects that you know to check ISMP for the latest and greatest. You can answer this way:

In the outpatient setting, tall man lettering and making sure drugs with similar names and strengths are not stored together helps reduce dispensing errors. Doing readbacks of verbal orders is also helpful. If there is ANY question about the prescription, I call the provider. Every single time. It's not worth it to risk harming the patient, even if he or she is upset about having to wait a few extra minutes.

In the inpatient setting, it helps to follow the recommendations by ISMP and the Joint Commission. Avoid trailing zeros; avoid certain abbreviations like QD, MSO4, and U for once daily, morphine sulfate and units. Again, ensuring to confirm and read back all verbal orders is essential. I have also heard of methods such as the STAR system (Stop, Think, Act, and Review) before verifying an order. This helps to make sure that I won't make an error in a stressful situation.

BLOCK 6 – COMMUNICATION AND TEAMWORK

In a day, the interviewers are trying to see what kind of a teammate you're going to be. You can be a great applicant with significant clinical knowledge, but if you're a pain in the butt to work with, they'll pass. They want to know that you are good at speaking to patients, others, and working within a team. There's always more to do; will you and can you do your fair share? Your answers to these questions will help them sort it out.

51. How do you resolve conflict?

For any conflict, whether it is interpersonal or not, make sure that there's a resolution. Most importantly, with questions that deal with personal conflict, be sure you're not blaming the other person and saying it's his or her fault. Take ownership of your role in the situation. Otherwise, you'll come across as someone who blames other people for your problems. Let's look at a sample answer:

In my technician job before pharmacy school, another tech and I fundamentally disagreed with the then current workflow. We had a system for IV admixtures spelled out that we had worked on with the manager. There were roles and responsibilities for compounding that came from the set of rules.

The other technician never really bought into the system, so she started showing her dissatisfaction by not completing her responsibilities. I felt like I was stepping up to try to make sure that patient care wasn't affected, but it was very frustrating.It made for a long couple of weeks. It was tense. We talked infrequently, and it was uncomfortable.

How I dealt with it was to go to her to figure out the root issue. She said she didn't like the workflow. She wasn't going to do it. I wanted to snap back, but I didn't. I said, "Okay, let's work with something new." We came up with something that we both thought was fair. The manager loved it and agreed to it. We're not best friends, but we were able to work together amicably from that point forward. So, I resolve conflict by findinga problem's root source and offeringa compromise to resolve it.

52. Can you give us a specific time you dealt with conflict as a leader?

I'm going right into an example with this one, but you need to be the hero of your own story.

Recently, because I had worked my way up in responsibility as an intern, I was placed in charge of the technician scheduling. I think they chose me for that position because I get along pretty well with everyone and I'm reliable. But my friend, a classmate who I introduced to the position, decided to go away on a weekend day for which I had him scheduled. There was no one else available to cover, and I too was going be away that weekend.

I consulted with my pharmacy manager and was able to get time and a half for that shift so someone would cover it, but I felt my friend had put me in a tight spot. He assumed because we were friends, we had the same relationship at work that we had outside of work. It was then that I realized I'd made an assumption that I shouldn't have. I was able to make a clear split between my work responsibilities and friendship; my friend wasn't. What I learned from that conflict was the importance of perspective. I need to make sure that I clearly understand the other person's point of view when I'm making assumptions if I want to get the desired result.

Conflict happens, but knowing that you are someone who finds a solution is key.

53. How do you get along with others?

You want to highlight your ability to empathize, make friends, and read off the occasional quote from Dale Carnegie's *How to Win Friends and Influence People*. Here's a brief sample answer:

There's an expression that "two shorten the road," and I'd often rather work with someone than go about something alone. I know I'm not going to be best friends with everyone I ever work with. I recognize and appreciate diversity in cultures, customs and personalities. I understand that everyone has a story. I realize too that everyone has a life outside of school and work. Everyone has his or her own trials and tribulations, so to speak, and I truly comprehend that. I just treat everybody as I would like to be treated. I always try to be helpful and cheerful, and I never hold grudges.

Again, it's about honesty. Don't say "I get along with everyone," when that's a very tough answer to believe. The interviewers want to know they can trust you and that you make the effort to play nicely.

54. How do you handle people who don't get along with you?

You want to be clear that you are someone who tries to get along and doesn't hold a grudge. Here's a story that illustrates that point.

There was a technician who had worked in the hospital for quite a while. As soon as I came on board, it was clear from his body language and abrupt answers that he really didn't like me. About a week in, we were both in the break room together, and I just said, "Do you mind if I ask you what I did that might have upset you so I can apologize?"

His response was immediate. All you pharmacy students get paid more than we do as soon as you're hired. I've been here everyday for four years and I don't make close to what you earn working part-time. Not only that, you were given computer-related assignments within just a couple of weeks of working here. It took me almost a year to be able to work with a computer; I was mostly counting pills.

So, I shared a little bit about my backgroundwith him. I told him that my family was so poor wehad to use sheets on the windows instead of curtains. I didn't apologize for being a student, but I told him that I too had faced challenges, only in a different way. I explained that I had to work this job, whereas some of my classmates didn't. I went on to tell him I know what it feels like to be treated in a way that seems unfair. And that was it; things got better between us. Although we didn't become best friends, we were able to air our frustrations and develop a mutual respect for each other.

That class difference, between technicians and pharmacists, between lab coats and scrubs, who sometimes do the exact same thing, counting pills, pulling meds, doing IVs, can be a source of tension. But the key is to make sure you're clear you're all on the same team.

55. How do you handle opposing opinions?

I've seen every answer to this kind of question and the takeaway is that you want to be easy to work with. Here's a practical response.

There's an expression that "it's often a person's mouth that broke his nose." What I mean is that talking without thinking or really understanding the other person can lead to trouble that can be readily avoided.

When the issue impacts patient care, for example, I try to find common ground and figure out exactly what points we disagree on as well as what we might agree on. I've found that often we're coming from the same place and have the same end goal – to take care of sick people. Maybe the other person has a different idea on how to get to that goal or a different angle. I really try to zoom in and understand the differences in order to achieve an amicable resolution.

Often there isn't one best answer. The interviewers want to know that you're not going to sulk in a corner if you don't get your way. They especially want to know if you're going to be combatative. Presenting a cooperative personality is ideal.

56. How do you deal with disagreements?

I fire the people involved, or if I'm not in a position to fire them, I tell on them.

Obviously, your story can't imply that you'll take either of these actions, so any type of answer suggesting that you would exhibit vindictive behavior is a big no-no. You might think you've told a story about a right made wrong, or that you were winning an argument, but you are really telling the interviewer, *"Watch out because I won't back down, and worse, I'll tell your boss on you."*

Here's a good general answer to the boilerplate disagreement question.

Bill Gates says, "Your most unhappy customers are your greatest source of learning." And I think this applies to unhappy patients as well. I believe that only about 10% of customers complain, although I'm sure it seems like more. But if you really listen to their complaints, you'll discover that they are not personal;they'reusually about systems that can be fixed. If everyone agreed with me, that'd be neat for a while, but I learn a lot from others' perspectives. I'm from Washington, D.C., so I grew up with people from many different cultures. I don't take disagreement personally, but I do take a personal interest in it.

Showing you have a growth mindset with disagreement is a relatively good path to go down.

57. You ever have a problem with a physician?

This is tricky. You may not have had this yet as a student. You've certainly had interactions with doctors, but never been turned down on a recommendation like a freshman asking a senior to prom, right? We're in a weird sort of spot with our profession as we don't have an ultimate say. Since it's a vague question, I might go relatively light on the answer and not put a patient's life on the line. The interviewer's lobbed you a softball; it's okay to just knock in a single. Try an answer like this:

Once, I was on rounds with the team, and my preceptor was called to a meeting, so I ended up rounding by myself that day. The doctor wanted to start a new medication, apixaban, as the patient had A-fib. She was 82 years old, and he asked what the dose should be. Honestly, I think I was a little too sure of myself, but I gave the doctor the dose that you would typically give for treating VTE, not for A-fib.

Later, I reviewed the recommendation with my preceptor, and it was a big deal. Obviously, it would have caused us to over anticoagulate the patient's blood. I had to rush back to the doctor who wasn't happy when I told him. Luckily, we had only given one dose. It was challenging for me to go and own up to a mistake like that, but the doctor understood. It was a valuable lesson for me to learn regarding the importance of double checking when you're not positively certain, rather than guessing. That day I wasn't carrying my laptop with me, so now I always do in order to have my references handy.

The interviewers are not expecting you to be perfect and would be a little miffed if you presented yourself that way. Showing you learned from that mistake shows a lot of courage.

58. Did you ever run into a disagreement with a doctor?

This begs for an example first.

As a student, I don't have a lot of direct contact with physicians, but I do remember a time when I called the doctor's office for a switch. The nurse answered, but as soon as I started talking about switching one HMG-CoA for a preferred one the physician got on the phone and tore into me. She said, "I know what's best for my patient and what medicines she needs." Her response took me by surprise and I remembered what my chief pharmacist had said. He had told me that when you get attacked, start your answer with "I understand" which does not mean "I agree", and then present a "would you rather scenario" requiring an "either-or answer." So, I said, "I understand" and just kind of rolled with it. My answer sounded something like this.

I understand you must receive many requests like this by phone or fax, and maybe you've gotten a number of these just today. Would you rather I ask my pharmacist or the patient to talk to you? I know you're frustrated with the insurance companies, and it seems I might be making things worse. Then I just shut up and listened. For a minute the doctor said nothing, but then said, "I know this patient will not be able to afford the medicine if I say no, so go ahead and change it. Thank you." And that was it.

You're going to be working with doctors at your residency, but if you mess up, it's the residency director who hears about it. He or she wants to know if you're going to be an asset or a liability. Clearly showing you can handle a direct attack demonstrates you're likely on the asset side of the balance sheet.

59. Tell me about a mistake or "war story." How did you handle it?

This references instanceswhere you've had to go back and fix a mistake made by another health care provider. An example would behaving to correct an inappropriate antibiotic regimen prescribed by a Nurse Practitioner or Physician Assistant.

Be careful - you've just been baited. Proceed with caution. Despite what it seems, this question is NOT an invitation to tee off on the incompetence of another health care professional. If your answer to this question includes a healthy dose of "professional shaming," you will come across as petty and difficult to work with. Instead, steer your answer toward a more empathetic and constructive path. Here's an example:

On my acute care APPE, a practitioner ordered metoprolol 50 mg BID for a patient whose heart rate was 46 beats per minute. When I brought it up to him, he explained that he was restarting the patient's home medications to be compliant with recommendations from the Centers for Medicare and Medicaid Services (CMS) and the Joint Commission. I explained that I understood his reasoning, but still thought it would be better to wait until the patient's heart rate returned to normal. I also recommended trying a reduced dose to help prevent future incidents of bradycardia. Eventually, the practitioner agreed, and we held the metoprolol for a couple of days before restarting at 25 mg BID. My preceptor for the rotation mentioned that she was proud of how I handled the situation.

For information on the pitfalls of professional shaming, you can find a post on TLDRPharmacy titled <u>The Epidemic of Professional Shaming</u>

60. What's the pharmacist'srole in the health care team?

You and I both know we are the drug experts. Your interviewer knows we are the drug experts. And every single interviewee who answers this question will answer it somewhere along the lines of "Pharmacists are the drug experts on the health care team." Don't do that. That's not going to help you stand out. Instead, answer it with something like this:

In my opinion, pharmacists serve a vital role as the communications experts on the health care team. I like to think of us as the "translators." Our job is to converse with people with varying degrees of health literacy and to help them make informed decisions with regard to their medicine. On any given day, we may be offering a dosing recommendation to a physician, taking a verbal order from a Nurse Practitioner, helping a nurse calculate a drip rate for a heparin infusion, or explaining to a 65-year-old patient what atrial fibrillation is and why she needs to take an anticoagulant. Those demands are unique to our profession, and I think it puts us in an excellent position on the healthcare team.

For more reading about the role of a pharmacist, check out two articles from TLDRPharmacy:

How to Be a Successful Pharmacy Resident and

The Pharmacy Profession is Moving on With or Without You

BLOCK 7 – COMMUNICATION AND TEAMWORK CONTINUED

This group of questions will continue for what will seem like a very long time. It's not that the interviewers don't care about what you know; it's how important 'fit' is when it comes to selection. They sometimes have a dozen or more applicants from whom to choose during the interview process. They want only the cream of the crop. They want candidates who are clinically sound, good team players, and great communicators.

61. How do you earn your peers' respect?

You don't want to be a tyrant. You have to toe the line of not getting walked on and yet come across as a genuinely amiable person who tries to do his or her best. Your answer should go something like this:

I understand thattrust and respect are earned. So, if I haven't yet earned trust and respectfrom a peer, it's something that I'm going to keep trying to do. I realize that it takes time, but I want to win trust and respect primarily for my work ethic and for doing what I expect of others. Through consistent hard work, an attitude of let's get this done together, and a welcoming demeanor, I feel I will earn thetrust and respectof my peers over time.

It's okay to talk generally here as trust isn't something that dings when it's earned. Really, you're outlining your philosophy on the subject.

62. A student one-ups youon a clinical question to a physician; how would you handle it?

The temptation is to ask if the student answered the question correctly, but this is really about how you deal with insubordination. If someone crosses you, do you get back at him or her? Because there are so many rabbit holes you can go down, simply answer the question directly. Here's what I'd say.

I recognize that most students are young, haven't been around very long, and aren't aware of just how small pharmacy is. Perhaps they're really eager. Either way, I would come from a position of recognizing there's a lot of excitement in becoming a health practitioner and would assume the student didn't do it to hurt me.

The key is to show you would take a forgive-and-forget approach. The pharmacy world is too small at a residency site to hold grudges and plan retaliation.

63. How do you handle a verified order for an infant that is ten times the usual dose?

You have a knee-jerk emotional reaction to this question, right? I don't know what the medication is and I'm not a pediatrics expert. Neither are you if you're a 4th-year student reading this, but let's look at what we have. You've been asked to give gentamicin, for example, at 10 times the usual dose to this poor little baby. What do you say? Try this:

I recognize I'm a student with minimal experience, particularly with pediatrics, and especially neonates. I know the literature is sparse for children because most clinical trials are not performed with them. And so, there's a lot of medicine that happens that's not in the package insert. I would have to be taught the right thing to do. Consequently, this situation would be a learning point for me.

I need to know, is this dose a standard practice at other places? We're in a hospital right now. Is this part of the hospital's standard operating procedure for this sort of thing? Is the attending around? Does she know what we're doing? Is my preceptor around?

In residency, you're going to be presented with knowledge that's new to you. But, the interviewers also need to know you can stand your ground, and be confident in your training. What they're really looking for is if you will ask for help when you need it and then ask again when it really matters, like with this infant.

64. You're asked to fill a medicine that doesn't seem quite right; what's your process?

This question is asked not only to find out what you will say, but also to reveal whether or not you'll have the courage to go head-to-head with someone who has a different opinion in order to safeguard the patient's well-being. A quick answer might go like this:

I would reiterate my concerns with it, but I feel like that might go into the data. I would also ask for a second opinion. I would explain that my intent isn't to insult him or her, but is to double check in order to be safe, rather than sorry.

The residency director wants to know the team has sound intuition. If you have an example of a save, you can put it here, but be wary of professional shaming.

65. How do you handle recommendation rejection on a routine med?

Please do not whine, cry or lose your cool. Keep it civil. Here's an example of how I would address this question:

I received excellent advice about rejection from long-term care pharmacist Eric Christianson who wrote the books <u>Pharmacotherapy</u> *and* <u>The Thrill of the Case</u>. *He shared that his first thought about rejection is to be respectful because you are in a small community and will be working with so many of the same providers over and over again. If I were dealing with a life-threatening situation, however, I would ask the provider to repeat the rejection, not because I hadn't heard them, but because I want to be sure this was exactly what the provider wanted; then, I'd document it.*

In fact, there's a story about a pilot and co-pilot who came from a culture where you never question authority figures. In this case, the pilot was the authority figure, so the co-pilot diluted the strength of his recommendation to the point where the pilot paid little heed to it. They both ended up dying because the co-pilot hadn't effectively communicated that they were about to crash. While we too have a hierarchy between the professions, I am always advocating for the patient, so we don't all crash.

66. How do you handle clinical recommendation rejection on a *severe* case?

At the end of the day, you are not in charge, and unfortunatelywe're still not providers, at least not at the time of this writing. What the interviewers want to know is if you know when to escalate and when to give in. So, the team did not accept your recommendation. You say,*"Well I researched really hard, I had checked it over with my preceptor, and we had these perfect sources; I based my recommendation off of this."* And still, the team didn't take it. What do you do? Answer with a specific recommendation like this:

Not too long ago, I wanted to decrease the dose for a patient. The patient was on a Zosyn infusion, and his renal function had tanked, so I felt we needed to lower the dose based on his creatinine clearance. My preceptor agreed with me, so I recommended the decreased dose to the team, but the doctor said no. He felt that the patient was too sick and he wanted the treatment to be more aggressive.

It always feels good to have your recommendations accepted, but at the same time, I understand that medically treating a patient is both an art and a science; it's not black and white. So, in this particular case, the physician felt he wanted to be more aggressive. I seized this rejection of my clinical recommendation as a learning opportunity. Honestly, I learned that in critical care patients Cockcroft-Gault is not the gold standard. There are just certain times when it might make more sense to push the envelope.

I haven't experienced a life-threatening situation, but in the case I just shared with you, I had done my research, yet the team decided not to accept it. I documented what I had recommended. I would hope that in a life-threatening situation the best result would come out for the patient, but again, I would turn the situation into a learning experience where we would all work together.

67. **How do you handle a medication error you caused?**

First and foremost, your answer needs to be that you'll own up to it. Whether it's an inpatient or outpatient issue, you'll also have to apologize. Otherwise, you'll lose the trust of your patient and peers by trying to sweep it under the rug. And lastly, you'll need to make sure that it gets documented.

Documentation is often the hardest part because there's something about writing it down that makes it feel like a confession, and that you're putting yourself in harm's way. But the penalty for not writing it down is much worse. First, if legal proceedings result from it, and it's discovered that you tried to cover it up, you'll be in serious trouble. Second, and this you should emphasize to the interviewer, is that if you don't document, we lose the opportunity to fix the process or system that caused the error, and that correcting your error might save others in the future. I'd put an answer like thistogether:

If I'm face to face with the patient and had just found out that we'd given him the wrong medication, I would, of course, own up to the mistake and apologize. And that would be the first and most important thing. The second thing I would do is document the error and report it to the internal committee for my institution or pharmacy. I'd want to investigate what happened that caused the error, and if it's a process, look to fix it to make a positive out of the negative. If someone hides or covers up a mistake, he or she may cause more harm because it could happen again. By being upfront, a faulty process can be fixed, possibly avoiding future errors for other patients.

68. How do you talk to the parents of a child whose medication you've filled incorrectly?

This question is really asking how you deal with caregivers when the patient can't advocate for himself or herself. Here's how I'd answer.

Ihave seen this happen many times, but there is one story that stands out. We received a call from a parent, and realized we had made a mistake.The pharmacist was very busy and said, "Please bring it in, and we'll exchange it." The parent hung up, and we expected him to come in, but as the day went on, he never came. So, I called and said, "I believe we made a mistake on your medication earlier, but we haven't seen you come in to exchange it. I'm calling to make sure you are able to come." That set off a tirade that clearly this should not be transactional, where the wrong medicine comes back, and the right medication goes to the patient. We knew him well because he came in all the time sincehis child had recurrent infections. I asked if the parent would come in, and also bring the child, since we wanted to apologize to both of them. I think this was a little unexpected, so they both came.

In allowing ourselves to answer in "busy mode," we didn't address the bigger issue, the emotional component that we could have harmed the child. When the daughter came in, she asked if she could get a toy "because of the mistake and all," and there was actually a kind of laughthat can only come from those unexpected things kids say. We apologized to both, gave the right medicine, gave back the money, and it worked out okay. I'll never forget that innocent "Can I get a toy because you made a mistake and all?" It was just a moment that really needed to happen; the emotions needed to be expressed before the actual transaction, the correct medication change, could happen.

69. Do you mostly lead or follow?

This is not necessarily a trick question, but you really don't want to pick only one with your answer. You want to demonstrate flexibility and growth. Consider this answer:

There's an expression that I feel fits here, You've got to do your own growing, no matter how tall your mother or father was. Although my parents were both successful practitioners in their own right, I had to find my own place. Yes, I followed them into healthcare careers, but becoming a pharmacist was my own path.

So, I guess it's situational as to whether I'm a follower or a leader. I tend to be more of a follower when I'm not yet competent in what I know or if it's a new situation. When I'm more comfortable, I tend to lead. For example, I was the leader on many group projects when I was in school. I had good relationships with my peers, and regardless of the topic, I could muster the troops, so to speak. So, I'm a little bit of both depending on the situation.

Now, I often intentionally put myself in situations where I am going to be a bit uncomfortable. For example, I chose an academic rotation where I knew I would be leading the class for many of the sessions and would have to speak in public. The preceptor modeled the teaching for the first classes, but after that, I did most of the speaking, and we worked together on activities.

I found that what made me a much more competent speaker was creating my own materials like PowerPoints and so on. When I tried to use previously-made materials, like old PowerPoints and published exam questions, the classes fell a little flat. When I had ownership of the materials, I felt more empowered and led better. So, when I do lead, I try to make sure I lean on my mentors and peers.

70. Are you a team player?

Most questions are open-ended with who, what, where, when, why, and how. From time-to-time, by design or mistake, you'll get a yes or no question. It is not to be answered with just yes or no. You should always expound on the answer.

Your answer to this has to be yes. Even if you're the only resident at the hospital, you are part of the healthcare team. No pharmacist can take care of patients by himself or herself. We need everybody on board. Even if you prefer working alone, or you will work alone a lot, your answer should highlight both. Here's a sample:

There are aspects of working alone I really enjoy. I prefer to study alone, and as I'm somewhat shy, I need my alone time. But I recognize that I can't perform my pharmaceutical duties by myself, and that as part of a team I can accomplish a lot more. Patient care is going to be a lot better with the physician, nurse, social worker and pharmacist working together. We have to work as a team, and I embrace that aspect. Even if there are parts of working where I prefer to work alone, I'm very comfortable being in a team. As I mentioned before, two shorten the road and make it enjoyable.

Block 8 – Communication and Teamwork, A Few More

It may seem like overkill, but communication and teamwork are really important. If the interviewers pick someone who doesn't pull his or her weight, is needy, or is difficult to work with, it makes for a very long year. They'll keep asking similar questions until they are sure you're not putting on a false front.

71. How do you contribute to your current rotation?

There is not a lot to sidestep here. Just make sure your role is not to do "whatever my preceptor tells me" or something like that. Tell the interviewers about what excites you in that rotation. If you're inanticoagulation, talk about measuring a patient's INRand dosing warfarin. Express your eager anticipation for communicating directly with the patients and explain how you relay their INR results, whether by phone, etc. Give them details on what you're doing without violating HIPAA about increasing, boosting, or holding doses and how you spent time on that. Talk about interprofessionalism and how you helped to coordinate with the surgeons. You can articulate you're *just* a student, but tell them how you've felt in the overall scheme with regard to growth. You can say something like this:

You can't plough a field by turning it over in your mind. I knew I wouldn't be competent right away, but I had to get hands-on experience to really learn what I did and didn't know with anticoagulation. I learned warfarin and rivaroxaban dosing basics, but I'm not really where I can manage a patient on an anticoagulant. I know we'll communicate about elective surgeries, diet, lifestyle modifications and when he or she will need to go to an ER, but I'm still checking often with my preceptor. My preceptor wants me to lead a journal club and that was an exciting milestone for me.

Zoom out and see the big picture. Even if it's a drug informatics rotation where you do a bunch of work yourself, show how you lead and innovate. Give a concrete number if possible like "*if this new process goes through, it could save the hospital up to one hundred thousand dollars because they're restricting an antibiotic."*

72. How do you deal with stress?

*Usually, I curl up in the fetal position and rock back and forth, bite my nails, and weep quietly. Then I go home and stress eat an entire box of chocolates.*Make sure you let them know you're kidding and that humor is one of the ways you handle stress, but you're still working on your timing.

For this question, try to maintain a level head and not let your emotions get the best of you. Maybe astressful situation is watching a patient code and potentially pass. Perhaps it's dealing with an angry patient because you misfilled their warfarin.Maybe you're butting heads with a coworker overa workflow that doesn't work. Your answer could go like this:

We're faced with stressful situations all the time. I try to maintain my center and to not get overly emotional about things that are outside of my control. I've found stressful situations have, in the past, made me grow the most, even when they're not enjoyable in the heat of the moment. Stressful situations don't cause me to crumble. I know they are temporary and that they too shall pass.

The answer doesn't have to be long, but should include that 1) you are human and get stressed and 2) you have techniques or resources to handle that stress.

73. Do you see a glass-half-full or half-empty?

Let's first talk about the false dichotomy question. When you've been asked an either/or question, sometimes neither answer is right, or it's more correct to use both. I would answer it in this way:

I would say that the majority of the time I see the glass half-full, but sometimes, when my energy is very low, I might see it as half-empty. However, I would actually look at the glass from a third perspective. I would say we're using a glass that's twice as big as it needs to be.

The occasional surprise answer can impact the interview more than you think. For you, this is the only interview you are doing there. For them, this is the same movie a tenth time. Give them a surprise or alternate ending as some DVDs do.

74. What's a tough break you hit during a clinical rotation?

Whatever the hardship, whether making an incorrect dosing recommendation and having to'fess up' for it, or conflicts with a coworker, you need to show how you've dealt with it and moved on. Here's an example where you show them what you do if you're clinically overloaded:

I was on this diabetes clinic rotation and to be honest, I had a demanding preceptor. I guess with my diabetes credential from pharmacy school, I thought I was ready, but this was a different level. I don't mean demanding in a bad way; instead, she's was one of the best teachers I've ever had. I had a lot of reading – papers and guidelines every night. I literally read through both the ADA and AACE guidelines. I'm not going to lie and say I slept eight hours peacefully every night, but the studying did make sure I slept. At the end of the rotation, I said something like, "That was intense." My preceptor said she knew I had done the credential and was excited that she could push me and that I responded.

There's going to be overwhelm or bad days. The interviewers want to make sure you're not going to let everyone know about *your* bad day.

75. Describe a time when you handled 'overwhelm' poorly at work.

This question is about owning up to one's own mistakes and being able to learn from them. It forces you to start on the negative and work your way to the positive. Here's a story I'd answer with.

We were absolutely getting killed at a retail pharmacy. Two technicians had called in, and since it was early in the year, insurances were changing. The pharmacist and I and the other two techs had a quick "what do we do?" huddle and agreed we couldn't do everything, so we decided to stop answering the phones and let them all go to voicemail. This allowed us to catch up, but then later in the day we received a visit from the supervisor, and started talking about what we had done.

While the conversation cleared the air about feeling that the front of the store hadn't supported us, we ended up doing what solved our immediate problem. This wasn't the first time it had happened; we should have addressed the issue long before it came to a day like this one. The better decision was to create a plan that gave us a procedure to follow for when we are overwhelmed; to plan for it, so to speak.

Again, you start with what you thought was right, then move on to what would have been a more positive or better solution.

76. How do you handle 'overwhelm' in college?

How do you still get good grades, but have time for yourself and maybe keep a job? There isn't a right answer here, but the answer should show that you are innovative and forward thinking (with a smattering of leadership!) Here's how I'd handle this:

The stars aligned and we had three final exams on one day, then two the day after that. My first thought was to look at my grades to see where I needed to study more for the lower grades, and study less for classes with higher grades. But, since I was in a study group, we decided on an alternate plan which was to create study sheets in a group.

Each would take a point role in reviewing a specific class that he or she was good at. Then we'd work together to study. We studied together right before a particular exam in a specific class. But we had never put our heads together like this, to handle multiple tests for multiple courses. There was definitely a feeling of accomplishment when we did better on our exams than expected.

Innovation plus forward thinking and some leadership equals a winning answer.

77. How do you handle things you *have* to do?

While there's a romantic notion of the residency during pre-residency, there are some realities that are a bit of a grind. This question is asking how you handle things you have to do. Clearly, you don't complain, and you do the best job you can. A way to talk about your student experience that transfers might be to talk about the rotations. I'd answer something like this:

The accreditation document requires that you do specific rotations. So, there are rotations that are clearly less interesting to me than others. That doesn't mean I put in any less effort, for the less interesting ones, however. I have found that regardless of the rotation, when less effort is applied patient care suffers, and to let patient care suffer is just not in line with my own work ethic. So, to answer the question, I put in as much effort into those things that I have to do as I do with tasks I really might prefer.

They are just looking to see if you'll go on this tirade about things you have to do. Keep it straightforward that you are a doer, regardless of how palatable a task is.

78. What's your worst retail pharmacy experience?

This is a trap. It's begging for you to slam retail as inferior and share complaints as if you are brothers-in-arms. But you're not on the same team, at leastnot yet. As with many questions, a pleasantly surprising twist to the answer makes it more enjoyable for the interviewer. I might flip the answer in this way:

I remember a hectic night at the pharmacy, and I compounded a liquid with multiple liquid ingredients and a powder. I did the math, the pharmacist checked it, and it went out. Usually, we leave compounds for the night pharmacist, but this patient needed a dose that night.

That script just stuck in my mind as we were closing up and I redid the math and found we had made a mistake. I showed it to the pharmacist, and it's, "Oh no, we really got that wrong!" We tried to call the patient, but he had no phone. We quickly compounded the new one, and I headed out to the patient's house.

I speak multiple languages and was able to articulate what happened and that we needed to switch the medication. We were lucky that he generally went to bed later than we closed, but that's my worst moment in retail. I think listening to your gut, and then responding as a team, responding quickly, saved us, but the fact that we almost harmed a child was terrible.

Showing that a bad patient experience created your worst day spins this question around with a pleasant end.

79. How are you a stand-out applicant?

Everyone is going to answer this with how hardworking and compassionate they are, and that their pharmacy journey began with a hospitalized grandmother who had suffered a heart attack. That's what inspired him or her to become a pharmacist. This might be true, but for you to stand out as an applicant, you want to talk about transferable skills. These are things like teaching guitar which is unique, interesting, and can apply to pharmacy.

You want to pick a memorable story and be unique like Dr. Seuss. Now apply that to pharmacy. That's the key here, not that you taught guitar lessons when you were 13 or 14, but why you are a good candidate because of that. In this example, I'll keep going with the guitar motif, but transfer it as I love teaching. Here's how I'd phrase it:

I've been as passionate about education as entrepreneurship. While I loved teaching, I charged for those guitar lessons earning $10 an hour. By the end of summer, I had just over $800, and I bought myself a new guitar with it. It took some problem solving to get the word out there that I offered classes, but it was being a 13-year-old who was trying to blend some natural inclination for solving problems with actually doing it.

As I developed my teaching style, it was all about meeting my students at their level. Instead of teaching the student the circle of fifths and the pentatonic scale, I taught a Green Day song that demonstrated the same fundamental principles. While I wasn't trying to create edutainment or add gamification to my lessons, I felt that sticking by the principle that I will teach as I'dlike to be taughtworked well. The same holds true as I educate patients about their medications; I'm excited to talk to them about their medicines, but I also take a systematic approach making sure I cover everything each time but in some way that meets them where they are. That's why I feel I stand out, I've been teaching for a decade and feel I'm an excellent entrepreneurial problem solver.

The main point of the book *Master the Match*, is that you need to stand out as an applicant and there are good and bad ways to do that.

80. What will your contribution be here?

This is just highlighting that you're a team player and that you recognize this is not the year of Y-O-U. This PGY-1 year you are an employee; you learn as much as you can and then become a clinical pharmacist somewhere. But how do you contribute? I would loop back to a desire to step up to the plate and articulate it like this:

I come from a large family, and I like to call my current workplace my classroom where my classmates are my extended family. The same is true with school, the community I live in, and hopefully this residency program – with everyone working together. I would do anything for my family. If I notice something needs doing, I'll step up to the plate and do it. I know this year is not just about me learning as much as I possibly can to become a clinical pharmacist; it's about contribution. I want to help. I want to do projects that matter.

I'm sure I'll be doing Drug Use Evaluations. I want to help find ways to save the hospital money, and, in doing so, pick up skills that will benefit everyone. It would make me sad to do a project to just meet an ASHP accreditation requirement. I want to complete a project that would make me feel proud that I was able to contribute something of value that will last long after I've left the medical facility.

Block 9 – Background Check, Sort of

Now that they know you care and can do the job, it's time for some fun. They can get to know who you are, what's unique about you and how creative you can be. Some of these questions are a little off-the-wall, but take them in stride and try to create pleasant surprises and twists. Most importantly, be a storyteller.

81. What are you reading these days?

There is no right answer, but it would make sense for you to talk about how reading either a non-fiction book is helping you to reach your goals or how a fiction book is somehow related to passions that you have. I'd actually "read" the same book for every interview that asks about it; you'll get better at answering the question. The one answer you don't want to give is, "I don't read anything that's not pharmacy related." It makes you seem one-dimensional and kind of obsessive. Try something like:

I listen to audiobooks in the car, and my most recent book is <u>How to Beat a Hydra</u> by Josh Kaufman; he's the same guy who wrote <u>Your Personal MBA</u>. I just like his narration style. The book is a fictional allegory, a lesson about dealing with adversity when you are trying to be creative or innovative. Each head requires a different approach to tackle and overcome. The hydra, or challenges, grow two heads when you cut off one. With his story, Josh is able to provide a lesson on perseverance in a very clever way.

Also, be wary of going off on a tangent with this one. They just asked what book you were reading, not for a chapter-by-chapter synopsis.

82. What do you do in your free time?

This is very personal, but as with other questions, try to transfer lessons to becoming a good resident. Here's one of our stories.

I tend to run at least one marathon a year. I work out every morning and some evenings; it re-energizes me to be around other people. I especially like CrossFit, a high-intensity workout program where a bunch of my cohorts and I get together to do tough workouts. With this program it's easy to scale things up or down so you can do handstand pushups or do them on your knees. That's what I do in my free time.

This is where you might find accidental comradery. If another resident is a runner or CrossFitter, they might ask some follow-up questions or give some advice about working out in town.

83. What do you do for fun?

This is a way you can sneak in another team player and leader reference. This is how I did it.

Whether it's a football game, basketball game or competing in intramurals, I like team sports. My favorite run is called Market to Market; it's a 75-mile, 8-person relay run from Jefferson, Iowa to Des Moines. I'm the team captain and while I organize which runner does which leg, I try to spread responsibilities like food, driving, etc. among my teammates. It's a 12-hour day that starts around 5:00 AM, but there's great satisfaction in finishing something hard with other people.

Do you see how I did that? Teamwork, leadership, and willingness to do 12-hour days all came together in the story that had nothing to do with pharmacy but everything to do with residency.

84. Describe yourself in one word.

The temptation is to use more than one word, but take on the challenge and think of it beforehand. You already know to use a positive word that fits along with your theme and what you want the interviewers to remember you by. Here's an example:

Persistent. I would definitely use that word. As a first-generation college student, I struggled to get through the pre-professional coursework. It wasn't that I wasn't prepared academically; I was able to take AP Chemistry and Pre-Calculus in high school, but the way classes were scheduledfor three days a week or two days a week really threw me off.

In high school, I went every day, and then played sports after school and on weekends. On Sunday nights I cleaned up and organized for the week. I didn't realize how important it was to get study buddies and work together since I was able to handle most academic challenges on my own. After a couple of semesters, I got a hold of things, but the classes became harder. It wasn't until my junior year that I came into my own when I was with people in my major.

Remember, it's not brag about yourself in one word, it's simply find something that someone would say about you. If you're not sure what your word is, take a look at your LinkedIn profile and see if anyone has commended you for a certain characteristic. Sometimes others see what you don't see in yourself.

85. What job would you have if you weren't a pharmacist?

You want to find a hobby or passion that fits into some of the residency duties. Here's my example:

I'd still be teaching. Whether to middle schoolers in science or in test prep, I would be in front of students passing along what I know. Even if I were in business, I would still look for some position like a corporate trainer where I would have significant teaching duties. Just putting my energy into sharing what I know with other people is something I really enjoy. So, I'd be in sometype of teaching profession.

This question allows them to round out their evaluation of you. They want to know you really enjoy what you'll be doing next year at the core. If you're going to a residency with a strong tie to a college of pharmacy or a teaching certificate, this answer strengthens your position.

86. Who was your favorite professor?

There are some obvious answers to stay away from: admiring someone for his or her easy grading, how much fun he or she was at the bar at the end of the term, or how he or she was the one who told you to do a residency even though you didn't want to. Basically, picking a favorite professor is choosing who you hope to become.

My favorite professor was my ambulatory care preceptor. She knew every patient's name, spoke to them in multiple languages if needed, and was totally engaged when listening to them. Some people hear you, but don't listen. She really attended to each patient and just let them tell his or her own story. At first, you think it's inefficient to spend so much time getting the personal stories, but in the long run, you realize itis much more efficient to do it this way because you tend to get each patient's whole story.

Take a few minutes to think back as well to that professor and if you ever thanked them. If you didn't, consider writing a hand-written personal note. I know as a teacher, when my students contacted me after the semester to thank me, it was really special.

87. Academically, what are you most proud of?

This is your chance to show off a little bit, but remember only to show off a *little* bit. That person interviewing you might have had five times the success you had, so the humble brag is appropriate here. Here's how I would answer this:

I'm most proud of getting an article published in my state association's peer-reviewed journal. Three of us had worked on it over winter term as a writing project. I was most proud of it because we'd initially let it go as unfinished because we had to go back to classes forthe spring term after the winter seminar.

We asked the professor, "Can we revive this?" We've found that many writers intentionally put writing aside for a while to revisit it with new eyes later. After we restarted, it was a fresh challenge. So, reviving a project that was dead in the water and getting it published was a proud academic accomplishment.

Showing, through story, that you finish what you start is a strong transferable skill.

88. Outside of school, what are you proud of?

This is very personal, but make it show you are someone who works well with others and loves to lead.

Because I'm into fitness, I would say I'm proud of completing my eighth marathon. I'm not proud because I completed eight, or because I ran a lot; I was proud because I had completely changed the way in which I ran the marathon. I had been injured for most of the year, and had opted out of running this one. But then I decided to ask the question, how can I do it? I discovered that there was a technique of running for two minutes and walking maybe one minute and doing that over and over. It seemed counterintuitive to enabling someone to compete in a marathon, but it ended up that I finished in about four hours and 10 minutes. My best is three hours and 50 minutes, so I ran my eighth marathon only 20 minutes slower than my personal best. And I walked for almost 100 minutes of that long-distance race.

I was really proud of the fact that I took a situation where I was hurt and couldn't do things as well as I wanted to, and found and adopted a different technique that enabled me to get to the point where I could succeed. I would have liked to have completed the race in under four hours (an arbitrary number), but I was elated that I finished.

89. What medication would you be?

The big thing here is to recognize that the interviewers didn't ask which medicationsyouare *on*. Instead, they want to know something about you that reflects you abstractly, *and* that you are able toanswer a kooky question using a good story that actually makes sense. I'd answer like this:

While I believe a good laugh and a long sleep are the best cures, I'll commit my answer as fluoxetine. This drug was significantly misunderstood when it first came out because the media attributed a suicide to the drug. The story goes that someone killed himself because he was on fluoxetine. In reality, the patient was too depressed to commit suicide, but it was the fluoxetine that gave him the added energy boost that enabled him to go through with it.

However, I believe fluoxetine was a breakthrough. The TCAs anticholinergic properties are difficult for patients to tolerate. Also, there's the danger of prescribing it for suicidal patients. The tyramine interaction makes the MAOIs not the safest choice.

I don't know if that story is entirely true, but fluoxetine went on to replace TCAs and MAOIs, easing the suffering of millions of people. So, if I had to pick a medication, it would be fluoxetine, the drug that led the way to making a whole lot of people feel better.

Notice how the story not only reflects some rationale thought, but you can demonstrate a smattering of pharmacology pearls as well.

90. What's your favorite animal?

Again, this is just a fun question; don't get crazy with the answer.It's a way for you to express some creativity and show who you are. If I wanted to embrace my true nerd, I would be talking about magic-user familiars like cats and small dragons. But here's how I'd briefly answer the question if I were on my best behavior:

I'd like to be a bald eagle. I've flown on airplanes, and I've been on amusement park rides, but I've never had control over where I flew. I think it would be amazing to explore the world from the air and see how wondrousthe worldis from that vantage point.

Notice how the answer shows that you look at things from a different angle. Pick an animal, then expound the choice's best attributes.

BLOCK 10 – BACKGROUND CHECK, CONTINUED

Some of these questions can be experimental and some straightforward. Again, your interviewers want to build a unique picture of you. Help them determine your level of creativity and honesty, and add a pleasant twist at the end.

91. Why are you the best applicant?

You want to say, "*I don't know; why are you trying to trap me with a question that begs me to brag about myself in a way that makes me look like a jerk?*"Instead, use the humble brag here and combine it with 'fit' rather than test scores or papers published.

I'm the best applicant if after our meeting, you as a committee and I as an applicant, feel we're the best fit for each other. There's always going to be someone with a higher test score, more publications, or better-written recommendations. But I think it comes down to wanting to be part of this family for a year or two. Throughout the day, I've really loved what I've seen here and want to be a part of it; I hope you feel the same way. This is my number one choice.

A huge mistake applicants make is not saying outright, "I want to be here." Sure, you're going to rank the residency site, but the residency match scoring favors the applicant, not the site. Residency directors don't want to be turned down either. Making clear you are going to put them first makes clear your intention.

92. How have professional organizations helped you?

What you want to do is clearly make the question go a little longer to read: how have professional organizations helped you *to help others.*

I'd answer like this:

Professional organizations canmass resources. It's one thing to speak to a congressman or woman one-on-one;it's another to represent the interests of tens of thousands of constituents in a single unified voice.

Professional organizations provide resources that an individual might not have on his or her own, as well as access to influencers. The top-end speakers at the national organization meetings like Michelle Obama are costly to book, but with an organization, the membership can learn from these leaders.

I've been able to help others by leading my college's chapter and making some of my classmates aware of opportunities. We've networked at regional and national meetings and have volunteered in our community.

You can also get specific with the organizations you are involved in and the volunteer work you've done.

93. Can grades predict a resident's success?

There are two ways you can go with this one. If you have bad grades, obviously you're going to say no. The grades don't have much to do with your clerkships and performance. But what you want to say is that you often have to make trade-offs. You wanted involvement in organizations to be a better-balanced person. You needed to work to survive. While you want your grades to be better, you feel your practical experience in leadership was worth it.

If you have good grades, make sure to be careful about flouting that fact. Many students have good grades. I've heard residency directors in even the top programs say, once an applicant makes the grade cut or minimum, it's all about 'fit' from there. Grades are just a convenient way to reduce the size of the residency applicant pile. With good grades you can make the argument that they are a sign of hard work and consistency, but not that one applicant is necessarily better than another. I might answer the question in this way.

I think grades demonstrate a work ethic. However, I don't know that a cumulative score tells the whole story. Some people "get" college a bit later than others. For example, I didn't really understand college success until I was a junior in the smaller major-specific classrooms. I went to R-1 research colleges where I had 300 students in a lecture hall. But once I had that community, of about 25 to 30 students, it was a lot better for me. I think of grades as being 'feedback' rather than being good or bad.

94. You're stuck on a desert island and find a first-aid bag. What three over-the-counter drugs do you hope are in there?

This is all you, but can demonstrate your ability to learn drug classes. Remember, they are interviewing many people. Slow down and give them a good story. Just as my kids prefer that I make up a storywith these questions, they're hoping for a little nugget of entertainment in their day.

I'm not sure what's on the island for food, so I would definitely want something for GI distress like an antacid or proton pump inhibitor. I expect I'll be building myself a shelter and a raft to get off the island, so an anti-inflammatory like ibuprofen for aches and pains would be helpful. Finally, I would needsome zinc oxide to protect me from the sun's rays.

It's really about being creative and making logical choices. Show them you're someone that they want to have on their island.

95. How do you define a pharmacist committed to the profession?

There are a couple of ways you can answer this, but generally, action trumps words. If you had a leadership experience, pushed innovation and entrepreneurship, or helped in the community, that's what you want to highlight. The answer could sound like this:

I think a pharmacist committed to the profession doesn't necessarily have a specific job, but for whatever career he or she chooses, they have invested significant time and energy. I think there are outward and inward components to recognize. Outwardly, I was the president of my chapter for a year and am continuing to mentor the current incoming president to help her make the transition. I think a pay-it-forward mindset is key. I tried research with one of my professors, and even though our results didn't come out the way we expected, we realized we needed a different approach, and I'm still working on that. Finally, I've spent over 100 hours volunteering for this charitable organization because I've found that it really speaks to what I want to do outside of the pharmacy walls. While I know the PGY-1 year is both about learning and discovery, I see myself working towards innovation and entrepreneurship when I have the opportunity.

Inwardly, I've talked to other people who have completed this residency; they've said that they really gained a good understanding of who they were and what fit and what didn't. And when they went on to PGY-2, they had a perfect sense of their next steps. So, they could commit themselves to the profession because they knew their place in it.

96. What was the most recent peer-reviewed article you read?

Be careful with this one because if something you read wasn't recent, in the last year or two, it speaks poorly about how you stay current. The interviewer wants to know that you're not going to rely on your instructors, but that you'll take the initiative on your own and read articles that interest you.

You can also use this as a 'show don't tell' opportunity to talk about your future. If you have a PGY-2 in pediatrics coming up, then your article should focus on peds. Be careful using a journal club article; make sure it shows self-motivation. If you talk about an assigned journal article, make sure you talk about how you put the group together. If you chose the article, speak to why you chose that article. You don't want to give the impression that you only read what's assigned.

97. How do you push the profession forward outside the pharmacy school walls?

This is seeing if you are all pharmacy all the time in the building, or if you are really reaching out to make a difference. You can answer this with a political bent if you have been to a college's legislative day.For example:

I found out who my representatives in state and national office were. One of the senators had been in office for a long time, but my perspective, as a future health professional, is recent. So, the way I look at things is very different. He just won the last election, so I congratulated him and asked if I could talk with him, and ask some questions.

When I sat down one-on-one with him, I learned a bit about talking to an elected official and what information I should have ready. He explained the legislative funnel to me, and that expressing an opinion one way or another needs to happen as the legislation is reviewed. On one issue, I knew my opinion but didn't know the state association's stance on it. They ended up being the same, but it was clear that I needed to know what issues were most important to me and on which side my fellow pharmacists and I stood.

So outside of the pharmacy school walls, I'm starting to get an understanding of the political process. Right now, my role is to return that information to my classmates, but it might expand.

There is an expectation that you will advocate for the profession. Meeting legislators is a good way to do that.

98. What issue interests you most today?

One issue that's in flux and won't really offend anyone is that of 'fit'. Where do practitioners fit into an "outcomes-based" model? You can use a sports analogy with this question, but really it's more of a personal choice in answering.

Now, we grade patient care on outcomes. How does a patient do? Does he or she return to the hospital? Doeshe or she stay well? I'd like to use a sports analogy with a basketball team to answer this.

Generally, in basketball, there are three primary positions. There is a guard, or point guard, who may be smaller, but is quick and a good decision maker. There is the center who is usually very tall, and often is focused on defending the middle and taking opportunities from close to the basket. Finally, there are forwards, who are usually tall as well, who work around the basket. The 'take home' is that if you put five centers on the floor, you would have a great defense, but could they get back on defense around quicker opponents and so on?

The same is true in healthcare, but our roles are not so well defined. What part does the pharmacist, nurse practitioner, physician assistant, and physician have in providing and supporting the best patient care? I think that as a medication expert we're positioned to be an essential member of the team, but I also believe that the team has to be set up in a way that will allow for us to work at our very best.

99. If you were head of the largest pharmacy member organization, what problem would you tackle first?

This is also a personal one, but it examines how you would lead a large organization rather than a conduct a one-on-one interaction with a patient. It's more about getting to know how much you've thought about the big picture. I'd answer like this:

Our role clinically is relatively new. As recently as forty years ago, we weren't supposed to tell a patient what the medicine was for, the adverse effects and so on. Pharmacists made the drug and sold the medicine, so their role was tied to the product. Also, we were isolated. While physicians and nurses worked in tandem for centuries, we've just come on board in the same physical space quite recently. It's like we're a new player on a sports team. Can the established team trust us with the ball? What is our role? How do we best impact the team?

In an era of ever-shrinking services, we're one of the first places a patient now goes. How do we take on this role on the front lines? But we also miss many patients because they go to the aisle and don't come to us first. While self-care is convenient, it's unnecessary to take a risk with medicines when professionals can guide them.

So, the major problem, I believe, is one of branding. We are the first place a patient wants to go, but we are not the primary provider. We have a unique and team-based skillset, but the team of physicians and nurses that have been together for a long time may not know how to lean into us and work with us.

Think about where you want the profession to go, then work backwards to see the steps we need to get there.

100. Is there anything we haven't asked you that you'd like to talk about?

Again, you want to turn this around and surprise them. Give them something unexpected; show empathy for your interviewers. Make sure, if it is a choice you want, to make clear you want this residency. I would answer this way.

I'd like to use this opportunity to thank you and to tell you that I really appreciate the time you've spent with me today. I want you to know you that this residency is definitely my first choice and that I think we're a good fit.

Saying goodbye is as important as saying hello, if not more. You don't want the departure to be as awkward as that "should we kiss or not" as you leave a first date. A firm handshake, a smile, and a thank you go a long way.

Block 11 – Questions You Should Ask

What to watch for:

Look carefully for nonverbal cues. For example, if the current residents look like zombies, take that as a sign that they are burnt out. We should also note not to ask ALL of these questions. Select a few that are important to you, and let the conversation guide which questions you use. Try not to sound like your reading off a list of questions that you ask everyone. Still, bring the list if you aren't sure you can remember what you want to ask. Is more important to get your questions answered, you don't want to pepper them with emails after. Switch up the wording to make them seem unique and conversational.

I think it's also important to focus also on questions NOT to ask. For the most part, this is anything that can be found by a Google search or from the main residency website. So, don't ask "What are your required vs. elective rotations?" and so on. By the way, we address this in Mastering the Match.

Drawing Dead

I wanted to explain the concept of drawing dead. In late night Texas Hold-em tournaments, you'll sometimes see 100% to win under one hand, 0% to win under the other, yet the players are still drawing cards. The person who has a 0% chance to win is "drawing dead," drawing against a hand that cannot be beat.

In these interviews, there is an idealistic feeling of fairness. That each resident interviewee will present him or herself and a fair judgment will be rendered as to where to rank that applicant in the match.

However, accredited sites must interview applicants regardless, even if they know they have someone they really want. If you're drawing dead, you'll see the exhaustion in the faces of those who are interviewing you. This may be fatiguefrom having to keep interviewing, even though they are fully aware an applicant before you locked it up. Or maybe they had a student for 20 weeks that they fell in love with on an extended APPE. But, they can't be 100% sure, so they interview and interview.

You want to do two things. First, recognize that all you can do, is let them know that you'd love to be there so they rank you as high as possible. You never know, their "lock" might have a *Bachelor in Paradise* moment and find love with another residency site unexpectedly. Or, circumstances would make it impossible for that person to accept the match there after all. The second thing to recognize is that body language, vibe, and that 6th sense needs to be on high alert. Feeling like you fit goes both ways. If something tells you things just aren't going to work out, take that into account as you make your choices. While many students will rely on pro/con lists and Excel spreadsheets to logically make a choice, ultimately it comes down to feel and fit.

There is a rubric in Master the Match to help you make a decision on where to rank.

Alright...questions TO ask...

To the residency program director:

1. How much flexibility does your program offer regarding rotation offerings?

Even if there's not much flexibility, it could still be a great experience. It's nice to know how this site compares to others you will interview with.

2. Can rotations be changed throughout the year?

As your needs or wants shift, can the residency move along with that? While the PGY-1 is a broad experience, almost half started in the last 5 years. These may be a little more malleable as they implement the program itself.

3. What are some clinical initiatives the department is currently working on?

This is a good one to ask while they are asking clinical questions. Again, it's better to ask during the interview to make it more conversational than at the end. Having a list of questions allows you to cross them off as you go.

4. What are some operational initiatives the department is now working on?

Will you be in the middle of an EHR changeover? Will they implement some new AI technologies? This question allows you to get a feeling of where the department is going, but also new jobs that might come available.

5. How involved is pharmacy in med histories and discharge counseling?

Some institutions employ other health professionals in this role. It's a good barometer for how well pharmacists are regarded as medication experts.

6. What are some past residents' research projects? What resources are available to help them, such as a statistician or research review committee, to ensure projects are valuable and well designed? Are these research projects chosen by the resident, assigned, or a bit of a hybrid?

Your project is a large part of what you will doing and carry forward from the residency. In my residency, I had faculty members who could walk us step-by-step through the math. We also had a writing group that met regularly and feedback from faculty as to the quality of our abstract. Don't feel like you are being needy here, you want this support and to know, in general, what projects make the cut.

7. How is information about departmental changes communicated to staff?

This question shows you care about communication and that you are interested in what's happening in the department.

8. How many residents have stayed with your institution in years past?

Knowing if this is a place where they hire their own can be a very important part of your decision. While this can change as the tides of departmental budgets do, seeing past residents as employees is a good sign.

9. What are the past few years of residents currently doing?

This both asks if they keep up with their past residents and again, if the institution hires them.

10. When was the last time ASHP visited for accreditation? Was there anything they said you needed to change?

This might be a little uncomfortable to ask, but it shows they are working to continually improve themselves. It's the reverse of asking the interviewee, what are your strengths and weaknesses.

11. If you could change one thing about your program, what would it be?

Another turnaround question that allows them to show they are human as well.

12. Have past residents ever made suggestions for change/improvement to the program? What did you do with their recommendations?

You want to be part of a family that works with you, not against you. Is the department rigid and uncomfortable with change, or innovative and receptive to it?

13. What do you look for in a residency candidate?

Another fun turn-the-tables question. You can use it just after they ask you a similar question.

14. *What sets your residency program apart from other programs?*

You may actually get a question back from this. They might first ask, "What do *you* think separates our program from other programs?" Answer thoughtfully but also conversationally.

To current residents:

1. If you could go back in time and choose this residency again, or another one...would you still be here?

You might think this answer is a lock, but they may be honest that it didn't meet their expectations. That doesn't mean it's not right for you, but it lets you know that they will be honest with you as well.

2. Do you feel like you could go to another clinical setting and comfortably function as a pharmacist?

This is ultimately what you want to get out of it. While it is a yes or no question, you'll still want the resident to expand their answer.

3. Is the program receptive to your feedback?

Body language will be a big one here. They may say yes, but their facial expressions might convey a different answer.

4. What has been your favorite rotation? (I'd recommend AGAINST asking about their least favorite rotation)

This gives them a chance to talk about their futures and what they hope to do with their career. It keeps the conversation going and puts them in the spotlight. They will remember that you were genuinely interested in them.

5. What (if any) fun things around here have you been able to do with your busy schedule?

You want to know that there are activities outside of the residency. Burnout will be readily apparent and if they can't answer positively, you'll want to make a note.

6. What would you change about this program if you could?

This isn't a bad question, it's just asking what improvements you could be part of. It's not asking would you change programs, rather, it's saying, what can we work on together. If you feel you can be part of that change, say so.

7. What advice would you give me as an applicant for this program?

This is a good final question. There are always aspects that certain sites prioritize and knowing these can give you a slight advantage.

FINAL NOTES

We're both very busy dads who made time to create a hundred questions and answers. Even if you think you don't have time, I assure you the time you put into preparation is well worth the effort. It all comes down to six words as an interviewee. *Tell a story; make a point.* If you tell great stories, with elements of emotional investedness, the interviewers will remember you, and you could go to the top of the list.

While the end of the book is here, the end of learning is not. Everything we write and create is meant to speed your knowledge of a topic whether clinical or not. We hope you'll take time to check out the resources on TLDRPharmacy.com and MemorizingPharmacology.comthat we pointed to in this book and continue to strengthen your chances for a *Strong ResidencyInterview*.

ABOUT THE AUTHORS

Brandon

Brandon Dyson, Pharm.D, BCOP, BCPS

Works as a Clinical Pharmacist and as an Adjunct Assistant Professor. He completed a PGY1 Pharmacy Residency at a major academic hospital. He can be reached at brandon@tldrpharmacy.com

Tony

Tony Guerra, M. HCI., Pharm.D

Teaches college chemistry and pharmacology. He's authored nine books and published four more. He loves helping authors bring their words to audio. You can find him in Ankeny, Iowa with his wife and triplet daughters. His best contact is aaguerra@dmacc.edu

Saying goodbye is as important as saying hello, if not more. You don't want the departure to be as awkward as that "should we kiss or not" as you leave a first date. A firm handshake, a smile, and a thank you go a long way.